AGENT'S DETAILS

NAME Wendy Stewart

ADDRESS 72 Bunderg Road

Douglas Bridge STRABANE

CO' Tyrone BT82 8QQ.

Tel no: (016626) 61487.

MY POWER WORDS FILE

ISBN 1 84030 027 2

Ambassador Publications
a division of
Ambassador Productions Ltd.
Providence House
16 Hillview Avenue,
Belfast, BT5 6JR
Northern Ireland

Emerald House
1 Chick Springs Road, Suite 203
Greenville,
South Carolina 29609, USA
www.emeraldhouse. com

DEDICATION

For Anna-Michael and David

THANKS

My sincere thanks are due to:-

My sister, Cherith, who transformed my handwritten script into clear type and created the layout in preparation for printing. Her advice and guidance with this task, along with her time and patience, have been invaluable to me.

My mother, who had the unenviable task of proof reading the script and who, along with my father, encouraged me to transform my initial idea for the book into a reality.

ABOUT THE AUTHOR

Rhonda Paisley is the second of five children born to Ian and Eileen Paisley. She is by profession an artist. She studied Fine Art at BJU, Greenville, South Carolina, USA, graduating in 1981 with a BA in fine art and minor in English. She also took a certificate course in Victorian art and literature at London University and holds a T.E.F.L. certificate. Her paintings have been shown in solo exhibitions in the United States, Belfast and Dublin.

For five years Rhonda worked among Belfast's unemployed young people and drug addicts. During this time she ran a drop in centre in Belfast where she held a seat on the City Council for eight years.

Currently she is involved in research work and is a part-time lecturer in Art and Design. She also continues her work as a painter.

INTRODUCTION

Can God Fly?

It is the easiest thing in the world to talk to children about God. The difficult thing is to talk with children about God. When God is the subject of your conversation then it is beset with difficulties not easily overcome.
One summer afternoon my nephew, then three years of age, and I were engaged in choosing which ice lolly he would like best when he looked up to me and asked, “Can God fly?” Not knowing where this question came from nor where it may lead, with much caution I answered that I believed if God needed to fly, He could.

“So where does He put His legs when He flies?!”

Such is the wonderful mind of a child. I do still wonder where God might put His legs if he did fly - or should that be when he flies! I won’t tell you my answer lest every theologian descend upon me, but it made us both laugh.
This book is an attempt to put into simple language some words and concepts which children come across in the Scriptures and hear from the pulpit and which in their complexity are difficult for even the wisest of God’s grown-up children.

I believe the “bread” should always be broken small enough for little hungry ones to feed easily upon.

I am ever thankful that my parents did this for me.

Rhonda Paisley
Belfast.

BIBLIOGRAPHY

Bible Cyclopaedia; Eadie, John
Religious Tract Society,
London 1881

Christian Behaviour; Lewis, C. S.
Centenary Press,
London 1943

Christian Foundations; Paisley, Ian R. K.
Martyrs Memorial Productions, 3rd Edition.
Belfast, 1984

George MacDonald: An Anthology; Lewis, C.S.
Font Paperbacks,
London 1983

Westminster Confession of Faith
Jn. G. Eccles Printers Ltd.
Inverness, 1976

Crudens Concordance, Alexander Cruden
Lutterworth Press,
Guilford & London 1982

YOUR MISSION

Hello little disciple,
We have an interesting mission ahead of us. Our task is to discover the meaning of some unusual words. These words can be found in your Bible so it is a very good idea to have it handy - that way you can look up the words and discover other interesting things about them by yourself. Sometimes words sound a bit hard to understand but with a little detective work they can soon be sussed. Are you up to this task? Of course you are! Let's get started.

HERE'S THE PLAN

We will take each letter of the alphabet and seek to decode some words which begin with each letter. Then in the 'EXTRA INFO' section we will learn about some exceptional words which teach us what are known as 'CONCEPTS'. As a little disciple concepts are a vital part of learning because these are the whole ideas or views of important matters which concern us throughout our lives.

So let's commence our word search. This will be fun!

My power WORDS files

TOP SECRET

THE A FILES

TOP SECRET

FILE ONE

Amiable

WHERE CAN I FIND IT?

You can find this word in Psalm 84 verse 1. The Book of Psalms is in the Old Testament. It is the nineteenth book of the Bible and there are 150 Psalms. Psalms are hymns or songs.

WHAT DOES IT MEAN?

This word means LOVELY. Other words a bit like it are FRIENDLY and PLEASING. If you replace the word amiable with one of these words and read the verse again you will learn what the Psalmist means.

HOW CAN I USE IT?

You can use this word when you think about Heaven. Heaven is an AMIABLE city. It is a FRIENDLY city and a PLEASING city. Heaven is like this not only because it has been well designed and built with the best of materials, but because Jesus is there. The word AMIABLE should remind you of Heaven.

i Extra info go to CONCEPTS FILE 'T' Tabernacle

ASSIGNMENT [circle your answer]

■ Did you find Psalm 84 verse 1? YES NO

◆ How many Psalms are there? 12 84 150

▲ Two of these words mean Amiable, which are they? Lovely Ugly Pleasing

THE A FILES

CLASSIFIED

FILE TWO

Adversary

WHERE CAN I FIND IT?

There are two books named Peter in the New Testament - First Peter and Second Peter. They are the 21st and 22nd books of the New Testament. If you find First Peter chapter five verse eight you will locate the big word ADVERSARY.

WHAT DOES IT MEAN?

A person who is your ADVERSARY is your ENEMY. An enemy is someone who opposes or is against you. The opposite person to an ADVERSARY is an ADVOCATE. An advocate is someone who is your friend and who defends you. Throughout your life you will have friends and you will have enemies. But always you will have one chief enemy and one chief friend. Your worst enemy will be the Devil and your best friend will be God. The verse in I Peter 5:8 tells you how fierce an enemy the Devil is. He is so menacing he would eat you! Ugh!

HOW CAN I USE IT?

You can use the word ADVERSARY to remind you to be vigilant just as it says in the verse. When an enemy is about - look out! Be watchful! Don't let that big beast the Devil catch you or tempt you. Remember your ADVOCATE, your friend and defender, the Lord Jesus Christ. He will protect you. The Devil is no match for Him! Stay on His side.

Extra info go to CONCEPTS FILE 'P' Propitiation

SECRET

FILE TWO

continued

ASSIGNMENT [circle 'yes' or 'no' to these questions]

■ Did you find I Peter 5 verse 8	YES	NO
◆ Is the Devil my ADVERSARY	YES	NO
❖ Is God my ADVOCATE	YES	NO

1 1 2 3 3 2

CLUES

DOWN
1. An enemy
2. Your best friend
3. Someone who is against you

ACROSS
1. A friend
2. Another word for advocate
3. The 21st and 22nd books of the New Testament

THE A FILES

SECRET

Anathema

WHERE CAN I FIND IT?

Do you know where the First book of Corinthians is? It is the seventh book of the New Testament and it comes right after the book called Romans. In First Corinthians chapter sixteen verse twenty-two the word ANATHEMA is found.

WHAT DOES IT MEAN?

If a person or a place is CURSED it is assigned or reserved for SEPARATION FROM GOD. This is very awesome and sad. It means that God will never love that person nor dwell in that place. It will for ever be empty. ANATHEMA means God is FINISHED with the person who does not love Him and He will not go into a place where He is not honoured. You will see that the word which follows it in First Corinthians 16 verse 22 is also an unusual word. It is the world Maran-atha. That word means 'our Lord cometh' and it reminds us that Jesus is coming back to earth.

Extra info go to CONCEPTS FILE 'C' COMMUNION

HOW CAN I USE IT?

ANATHEMA is something you would never want to be. So this word ought to teach us how wonderful it is to love the Lord Jesus Christ. If we love Him we can never be CURSED or FORGOTTEN by Him. To keep ourselves loving Jesus we need to COMMUNE with Him. Commune

NEED TO KNOW

FILE THREE

continued

means to keep in touch. We commune with God by reading His words to us in the Bible and by talking to Him in prayer. If we do this we can never ever have the word ANATHEMA applied to us.

ASSIGNMENT [fill in the gaps]

- If I Love God I will never be Forgotten by Him
- Commune means to keep in Touch
- When a person or place is Cursed it is Separated from God.
- MARANATHA means "Our Lord Cometh".

THE A FILES

NEED TO KNOW

FILE FOUR

Anon

WHERE CAN I FIND IT?

Seeing as this is just a wee word let's look for it in two places! You can find it in the first book of the New Testament - Matthew - chapter 13 verse 20. Then look in the second book - Mark - chapter 1 and verse 30.

WHAT DOES IT MEAN?

This tiny word actually has two meanings. When you read the word ANON in the Bible it means IMMEDIATELY or STRAIGHT AWAY. That's nice and easy to understand, isn't it? Often you will come across this word in other things which you read. Usually it refers to the word ANONYMOUS and it will be written with a little dot after the letter 'N', like so - ANON. But in the two verses which you looked up in the Bible it simply means IMMEDIATELY.

HOW CAN I USE IT?

If you read the two stories in the Bible where this word ANON is used you will learn that in both it teaches us how quickly responses were made by those involved in the stories. Very often we need to be quick in our reactions and not old slow coaches who are behind in everything!

ASSIGNMENT [circle the correct meaning for each word]

■ Anon means	ALONE	SLOW	IMMEDIATE
◆ Anon. means	BEHIND	ANONYMOUS	AHEAD

TOP SECRET

FILE ONE

Blasphemy

WHERE CAN I FIND IT?

There are 27 books in the New Testament and there are 39 books in the Old Testament. Colossians is book 12 in the New Testament and it is not a very big book as it only has four chapters. Look for chapter three and find verse 8. The word BLASPHEMY is in this verse.

WHAT DOES IT MEAN?

The first thing we learn about this word is that it is something we must not do. We know this because the verse which you found in Colossians says we must 'put off' or not do several things, and BLASPHEMY is one of these things. BLASPHEMY is what we do if we insult God. God is completely good. He cannot be unfair. He cannot tell lies. He cannot be evil. To use words which say He is bad or dishonest or unkind is BLASPHEMY.

Extra info go to CONCEPTS FILE 'U' Unpardonable Sin

HOW CAN I USE IT?

Let's find the book of Exodus now. Exodus is the second book of the Old Testament. This book has forty chapters! It is a lot bigger than Colossians isn't it? Halfway through Exodus, in chapter 20 you will find the TEN COMMANDMENTS. In verse seven you can read the THIRD commandment which teaches us that we must not BLASPHEME. It says we must not use God's name as a curse word nor as a worthless name because it is of great value. It also says that we will be regarded by God Himself as

SECRET

FILE ONE

continued

being guilty of wrong doing if we do not regard His name with value. So, the word BLASPHEMY should remind us how important the THIRD COMMANDMENT is.

ASSIGNMENT [circle the correct number]

■ **How many books are there in the New Testament?**

12 27 32

◆ **How many books are there in the Old Testament?**

27 51 39

■ **Which Commandment teaches us about the value of God's name?**

1st 3rd 7th

◆ **Exodus is which book in the Old Testament?**

2nd 5th 12th

▲ **Colossians is which book in the New Testament?**

2nd 5th 12th

THE B FILES

CLASSIFIED

FILE TWO

Blessed

WHERE CAN I FIND IT?

Let's find the book of Romans. Romans is in the New Testament. It comes right after the book of Acts. It is the sixth book of the New Testament and it has 16 chapters. You want to find chapter four and verse 8 and the word BLESSED.

WHAT DOES IT MEAN?

This is a great word - it means HAPPY! There are all sorts of things which can make us happy and we can be happy for a long time or a short time. The Bible teaches us how we can be happy for eternity! This verse in Romans chapter four teaches us that we are HAPPY or BLESSED when God does not leave the blame and guilt of our sins on us.

HOW CAN I USE IT?

The word BLESSED is a great reminder of the smile of God. When you are happy you smile and laugh. God has smiled upon you with His plan of salvation. He has lifted all the blame of your sins away from you. He has washed away all the dirt of your sins. He has done all this by sending Jesus Christ, His son, to die for you. If that doesn't make you happy there is something wrong with you!

i Extra info go to CONCEPTS FILE 'R' Righteousness

ASSIGNMENT [circle the correct meaning of the word]

■ **Blessed means** **SAD** **HAPPY** **GREAT**

THE B FILES

NEED TO KNOW

FILE THREE

Buckler

WHERE CAN I FIND IT?

In the Old Testament the ninth and tenth books are called Samuel, First Samuel and Second Samuel. There are 55 chapters altogether in these two books called Samuel. If you find Second Samuel and go to chapter 22, verse 31 you will see the word BUCKLER.

WHAT DOES IT MEAN?

A BUCKLER is a SHIELD. Very often in the Bible God is called the SHIELD of His people. A SHIELD protects and so this word BUCKLER teaches us that God is our protector.

HOW CAN I USE IT?

The BUCKLER or SHIELD is part of a suit of armour. Armour also includes a breastplate, a helmet and a sword. All these things protect the warrior. The Bible teaches us that we are a bit like warriors. There are things which come at us in our lives which try to destroy us and seek to hurt us. But if God is our BUCKLER or SHIELD He serves to stop them even touching us!

ASSIGNMENT [circle your answer]

Find the book of Ephesians in the New Testament. In chapter six you can read all about this special armour. It starts in verse 14.

- ■ **Did you find the BREASTPLATE OF RIGHTEOUSNESS?** YES NO
- ◆ **Did you find the SHIELD OF FAITH?** YES NO
- ▲ **Did you find the HELMET OF SALVATION?** YES NO
- ◆ **Did you find the SWORD OF THE SPIRIT?** YES NO

THE B FILES

CLASSIFIED

FILE FOUR

Brimstone

WHERE CAN I FIND IT?

The book of Psalms in the Old Testament uses this word in Psalm number 11 and verse 6. The book of Psalms is the book before the book of Proverbs. Psalms are songs. Proverbs are sayings.

WHAT DOES IT MEAN?

BRIMSTONE is SULPHUR. Sulphur is pale yellow in colour and smells disgusting! The verse in Psalm 11 where you found this word BRIMSTONE tells us what God thinks about wicked people. He is so angry with them for doing evil that He is prepared to release this disgusting element upon them!

HOW CAN I USE IT?

Our sins are just like sulphur. They smell disgusting! BRIMSTONE is required to get rid of wicked people who love to smell disgusting. On the other hand the very next verse in Psalm 11, verse 7, tells us that God loves people who are good and showers them, not with BRIMSTONE but with His love!

ASSIGNMENT [fill in the missing 'S' words]

- **Brimstone is S** ulphur **and it S** mells **disgusting!**

TOP SECRET

FILE ONE

Cankerworm

WHERE CAN I FIND IT?

In the Old Testament there are a group of books known as the Minor Prophets. One of these books is named Joel. It has just three chapters and it is the eleventh book from the end of the Old Testament. The word CANKERWORM is in the fourth verse of the first chapter of this book.

WHAT DOES IT MEAN?

A CANKERWORM is a DESTROYING INSECT. It is sometimes referred to as a young locust or a hopping locust. Sometimes it is referred to as a caterpillar. When you read about any of these insects in the Bible they represent a huge number of their kind. Very often they were employed or used by God to show His anger when nations sinned against Him. LOCUSTS were used in the EIGHTH PLAGUE upon Pharaoh when he would not let the Children of Israel leave Egypt. When insects such as the CANKERWORM came together in large numbers or swarms they could destroy whole crops!

HOW CAN I USE IT?

Often we think that just one tiny thing can't do much harm. But a tiny insect can gnaw and chew so hard it can even destroy the foundation of a house - especially if it brings a few friends around to join in the party as well! The CANKERWORM was really a destructive wee beast! A lie might just be one tiny wee word - no instead of yes, or yes instead of no. But then

CLASSIFIED

FILE ONE

continued

its friends join in and it becomes a whole sentence and then a full paragraph and before you know it the truth is all eaten up and totally destroyed! The CANKERWORM teaches us how something tiny can become something treacherous!

ASSIGNMENT

■ **Can you find the EIGHTH plague in the book of Exodus? Try looking in chapter ten. Draw a big smile in the circle if you found it.**

THE C FILES

NEED TO KNOW

Castaway

WHERE CAN I FIND IT?

Can you remember finding one of the books called Corinthians? Well, if you find the first book of Corinthians which is in the New Testament (right after the book of Romans) chapter nine verse 27 has this word CASTAWAY in it. Verse 27 is the very last verse of the chapter and CASTAWAY is the very last word of the verse.

WHAT DOES IT MEAN?

CASTAWAY means REJECTED. If something is rejected it is not up to standard. It is SCRAP. IT is CAST or THROWN AWAY.
That's easy to understand, isn't it? Just split the word into two parts and you've got it - CAST AWAY.

Extra info go to CONCEPTS FILE 'J' Justification

HOW CAN I USE IT?

Nobody likes to be a reject! Many people in our world are considered rejects just because they are different in an unusual way. Often a reject is a very clever person whom others don't quite understand. Often a reject is a poor person on whom others don't wish to spend money. Often a reject is someone who has made mistake upon mistake and others no longer care to help them. And sometimes we cast away or reject things which are good for us because we just don't want to know! In the Bible we learn

TOP SECRET

FILE TWO

continued

about many men and women who rejected the kindness of God's love. This made them CASTAWAYS from Heaven and eternal life. God does not want us to be CASTAWAYS, He doesn't want to scrap us, He wants to take us in and welcome us to Heaven.

ASSIGNMENT [fill in the missing letters]

■ **CASTAWAY means C**ast **A**way

◆ **CORINTHIANS follows R**omans

▲ **These books are found in the N**ew **T**estament

◆ **God doesn't want me to be a C**astaway

THE C FILES

CLASSIFIED

FILE THREE

Charity

WHERE CAN I FIND IT?

Like all the words which we are learning the meaning of, there are many places where this word CHARITY can be found. However, the word CHARITY cannot be found in the Old Testament, just in the New Testament. If you look for chapter 13 of First Corinthians you will find the word CHARITY is used NINE times in these 13 verses.

WHAT DOES IT MEAN?

CHARITY means LOVE. It means a special kind of love. The type of love which is also KINDLY or BENEVOLENT. The word BENEVOLENT is used in relation to giving help to the poor and needy. When we read the word CHARITY we should realise that the love which it means has many aspects to it. The chapter in which you found this word nine times tells you all about the extent of love.

HOW CAN I USE IT?

The very last sentence in the chapter you have found tells us that CHARITY is the greatest thing that abides or dwells in us. We have FAITH which makes us trust in God. We have HOPE which makes us look forward to seeing him. And we have CHARITY which is God Himself because CHARITY you remember, is love and GOD IS LOVE. You can find this fact in the first book of John chapter 4 verse 8. (Look for I John and not the Gospel of John).

ASSIGNMENT [circle your answer]

■ Did you find 'GOD IS LOVE'? YES NO

◆ Which is the greatest? FAITH CHARITY HOPE

THE C FILES

SECRET

FILE FOUR

Conversation

WHERE CAN I FIND IT?

The book of Philippians is in the New Testament. It has four chapters and it is the eleventh book, coming right after the book of Ephesians. When you find Philippians look at chapter one and verse 27. The word CONVERSATION is in this verse.

WHAT DOES IT MEAN?

Nowadays when we use the word CONVERSATION we usually mean that we are TALKING to someone. However, in the Bible this word has a larger meaning than just HOW WE TALK to one another. It also means HOW WE LIVE OUR LIVES. Our CONVERSATION is our ACTIONS as well as OUR WORDS.

HOW CAN I USE IT?

It is very important to God that we behave properly. For example, He does not like us to say that we love Him and then use the same tongue to tell lies! He does not like us to think unkind thoughts about others. He does not like us to do hurtful things on others. He likes us to behave like CITIZENS OF HEAVEN and MEMBERS OF HIS FAMILY.
When you read the word CONVERSATION in the Bible, remember it means how you TALK to others and how you WALK with others. What you SAY and what you DO - both of these are our CONVERSATION.

ASSIGNMENT [fill in the gaps]

■ Talking and walking = my C onversation.

NEED TO KNOW

FILE ONE

Daysman

WHERE CAN I FIND IT?

The book of Job is in the Old Testament. It comes just before the book of Psalms, making it the eighteenth book. It has forty-two chapters. Find chapter nine and look at verse 33. Here you will read this unusual word - DAYSMAN.

WHAT DOES IT MEAN?

DAYSMAN is really another word for a GOBETWEEN. A go-between is someone who stands between two people in order to reconcile or bring them together. A go-between intervenes or acts on the behalf of another. The best word to describe this person is the word MEDIATOR. DAYSMAN is really another word for MEDIATOR.

Extra info go to CONCEPTS FILE 'P' Prayer

HOW CAN I USE IT?

Who is our DAYSMAN? Jesus Christ is. We learn this if we find the first book of Timothy in the New Testament. Remember there are two books called Timothy so be sure to go to the first one! Find chapter two and read verse five. Here you will see that Jesus is our MEDIATOR and in fact the only Person who can go between us and God. When you hear the word DAYSMAN remember it describes the work which Jesus does as He tells

CLASSIFIED

FILE ONE

continued

God, His Father, what our needs are. The reason Jesus can do the job of MEDIATOR is because He died for our sins. He took our place and was punished for us. Isn't it a great thing to have somebody like Jesus talking to God on our behalf!

ASSIGNMENT [circle the correct answer]

- **The person who is your DAYSMAN or MEDIATOR is**

GOD

ME

MY MINISTER

JESUS

THE D FILES

TOP SECRET

FILE TWO

Devil

WHERE CAN I FIND IT?

For this word we are going to go to the very last book of the Bible - the book called Revelation. This book has twenty-two chapters but you need to find chapter 12 and verse nine. In this verse you will find the word DEVIL.

WHAT DOES IT MEAN?

In the verse which you just found you will have read three other names which are also used to describe the DEVIL. Do you see them? They are THE GREAT DRAGON, THAT OLD SERPENT and SATAN. The word DEVIL itself refers to the SUPREME EVIL SPIRIT who is our ADVERSARY. An ADVERSARY is someone who is opposed to or against us. An adversary wishes to destroy. So the word DEVIL is the name of the most wicked spirit who wishes to destroy us.

HOW CAN I USE IT?

The purpose or aim of Jesus Christ when He came to earth was to destroy the works of the Devil. If you find First John (remember first, second and third John are all towards the end of the New Testament) and go to chapter three verse eight, here you read exactly this! Jesus Christ, the Son of God zapped the Devil once and for all when He rose from the dead! This of course means that the Devil tries to keep us from loving Jesus. He would prefer us to be one of his followers instead of a follower of Jesus.

FILE TWO

continued

No Way! Would you want to be on the side of a loser? I think not! Would you want to be on the side of evil? Far better to be a child of God than a child of the Devil.

ASSIGNMENT [fill in the missing words]

For this Purpose was the Son of God manifested, that He might Destory the works the Devil

THE D FILES

CLASSIFIED

FILE THREE

Diadem

WHERE CAN I FIND IT?

The book named Isaiah has 66 chapters and it is the twenty-third book in the Old Testament. Find chapter 28 of this book and the word DIADEM is in verse five.

WHAT DOES IT MEAN?

A DIADEM is a HEAD DRESS or a CROWN. Sometimes the DIADEM refers to a very ornate crown belonging to a prince or a king. Sometimes the DIADEM refers to a headband made of silk or linen. Sometimes DIADEMS had inscriptions on them. An inscription is just another word for writing. These inscriptions often told the reason why the DIADEM was given. An example of this may be the action of a hero in battle. This would be written on the CROWN or HEAD DRESS.

HOW CAN I USE IT?

In the New Testament we learn that CROWNS are given by the Lord to those people who love and serve Him. You can read this in the second book of Timothy in chapter four and verse eight. In a way we are competing for a crown. We have to strive to win one of these crowns just as warriors had to do in the past. The things we must fight against to win one of these crowns are temptations. Satan teases or tempts us to do bad things - to lie, to steal, to cheat, to not be kind-hearted. We need to obey God's laws instead, so that we will wear a 'crown of righteousness' or a

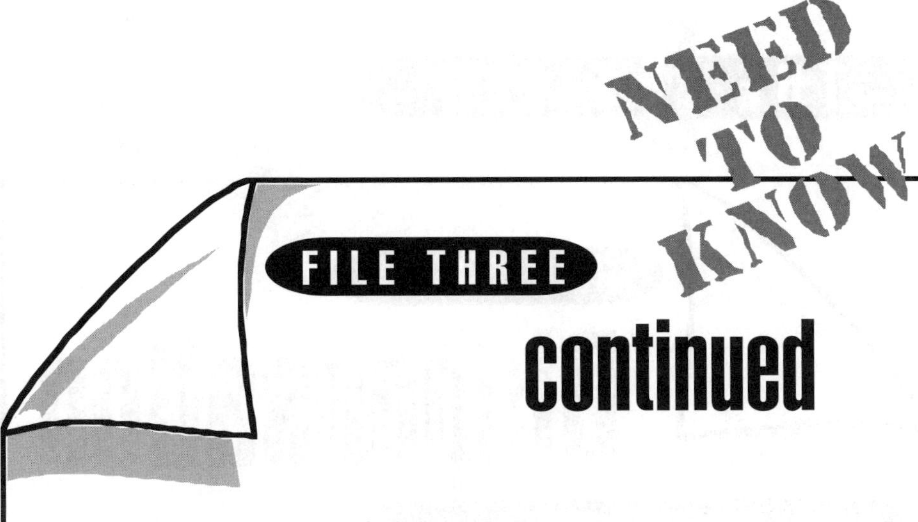

crown which has written on it the name of JESUS our SAVIOUR.
In order to become our Saviour, Jesus wore a very special crown. A crown made of thorns. This was to mock the idea of Jesus as a King. The soldiers who did this also put a reed in His hand for a sceptre and when we are striving to win our 'crown of righteousness' we should never forget the pain which Jesus suffered so that we could go to Heaven.

ASSIGNMENT [circle your answers]

■ **Some of these words can be used for the word DIADEM. Which ones are they?**

ROBE **HEAD DRESS** **SCEPTRE**

CROWN **UMBRELLA** **HEAD-BAND**

THE D FILES

TOP SECRET

FILE FOUR

Dispensation

WHERE CAN I FIND IT?

Ephesians is the tenth book of the New Testament and it has just six chapters. This big word DISPENSATION can be found in chapter three and verse two.

WHAT DOES IT MEAN?

It may sound like a very complicated word but in fact it has quite a straight-forward meaning. It means PLAN or SYSTEM OF GUIDELINES. Now, that's nice and easy to understand, isn't it?

HOW CAN I USE IT?

The verse you found in Ephesians talks about the DISPENSATION of the grace of God. If we replace the big word DISPENSATION with the little word PLAN it would read 'The plan of the grace of God'. This PLAN is of course the plan of salvation. And, when we accept that PLAN by asking the Lord Jesus to cleanse us from our sins we then seek to obey His other PLANS or GUIDELINES. These are guidelines such as the Ten Commandments. So you see the word DISPENSATION really covers the various GUIDELINES which God has put in place for our advantage and happiness. When we obey Him we are part of His plan too!

ASSIGNMENT [answer these questions]

- ■ How many chapters has the book of Ephesians? 
- ◆ Which word is another word for DISPENSATION? MAP 

CLASSIFIED

FILE ONE

Easter

WHERE CAN I FIND IT?

Acts is the fifth book of the New Testament, coming immediately after the four Gospels - Matthew, Mark, Luke and John. In chapter 12 of the book of Acts and in verse four of that chapter, the word EASTER can be found.

WHAT DOES IT MEAN?

EASTER is really another word for the FEAST OF THE PASSOVER. We often read in the Bible about feasts. These feasts were celebrations which marked important or happy occasions - a bit like a big birthday party! The FEAST OF THE PASSOVER was set up to mark the time when God PASSED OVER the families of Israel and did not kill their first-born children and creatures in the land of Egypt. You can read all about this awful event in Exodus chapter eleven (remember Exodus is the second book of the Bible). Jesus was celebrating the FEAST OF THE PASSOVER in what we now refer to as the LAST SUPPER. It was after this supper, during the night that Judas betrayed Jesus.

HOW CAN I USE IT?

EASTER is a time of much celebration for Christians. Christians are followers of Christ. Easter reminds us very much of the death of the Lord Jesus Christ and we are sad when we think about all the cruel things which were done to Him. But, on the third day Jesus rose from the dead!

NEED TO KNOW

FILE ONE

continued

It is this wonderful fact which we celebrate at Easter. Jesus is risen! Easter is a time of great happiness for us.

ASSIGNMENT [circle your answers]

■ **EASTER is another word for the feast of**

THANKSGIVING **THE PASSOVER** **SPRING**

◆ **JESUS rose from the dead on which day**

THE SECOND **THE FIRST** **THE THIRD**

● **The word EASTER can be found in which book?**

ROMANS **MATTHEW** **ACTS**

TOP SECRET

FILE TWO

Ephah

WHERE CAN I FIND IT?

You have found the book of Exodus a few times by now, so look it up again and turn to chapter sixteen verse 36. This verse contains this strange wee word EPHAH.

WHAT DOES IT MEAN?

An EPHAH is a measurement. It measures about 60 pints. So, if you got the milkman to deliver an ephah of milk you could probably fill the bath! The verse which you found in Exodus also gives you another unusual word. Did you spot it? The word is OMER. An OMER would be about 6 pints, as it says in the verse that it is just one-tenth of an EPHAH.
This word EPHAH has two other meanings as well.
1. It refers to A PLACE - you can find this in Isaiah chapter 60 verse 6.
2. It refers to A PERSON - you can find this in Genesis chapter 25 verse 4.
In fact Ephah was a grandson of Abraham.
So, Ephah can mean a measure of 60 pints, a place or a person. I wouldn't fancy being called Ephah myself, would you? You would be nicknamed 'Sixty Pints'!

HOW CAN I USE IT?

In the Bible there are all sorts of unusual words for different measures. There is this word EPHAH which we have just learned about and there is the word OMER which you now know too. Why don't you keep your eyes

CLASSIFIED

FILE TWO

continued

open for some of the others as well. Here are some which you could look out for:

■ **KAB or CAB**

◆ **HOMER**

● **HIN**

▲ **FIRKIN**

They all sound very interesting don't they?

ASSIGNMENT [circle your answers]

■ **Which of the following things can the word EPHAH refer to?**

A MOUSE **ABRAHAM'S GRANDSON** **A BATH OF MILK**

SIXTY PINTS **A MEASURE** **AN OMER**

THE E FILES

TOP SECRET

FILE THREE

Ephod

WHERE CAN I FIND IT?

In Exodus chapter 39 verse two you will find the word EPHOD. You should read the next verses as well, verses three, four and five as these will tell you some other things about the EPHOD.

WHAT DOES IT MEAN?

The word EPHOD really is another word for a CAPE. Not just any old cape you know, but a unique EMBROIDERED CAPE of very rich colours which was worn by the High Priest. The colours were gold, blue, purple, and crimson. Twisted linen was also used to make this cape and the shoulder pieces were held together by two onyx stones. These stones had the names of the tribes of Israel engraved or cut into them. Ordinary priests also wore capes or EPHODS but these were very plain in comparison to the one worn by the High Priest.

CRIMSON is another word for RED

Moses' Brother AARON was a famous HIGH PRIEST

WHAT DOES IT MEAN?

The EPHOD of the High Priest should serve to remind us of the beauty in which our great High Priest, Jesus Christ, is adorned. He is altogether

CLASSIFIED

FILE THREE

continued

lovely. His beauty is so incredible because He is Holy. He has never sinned, and can never sin. And remember, He takes His beauty and wraps it around us like a cape when we ask Him to be our Redeemer.

ASSIGNMENT

■ **Name four colours in the High Priest's EPHOD?**

purple ______ blue ______ gold ______ Crimson ______

▲ **Christ's beauty is His H** oliness

◆ **Jesus Christ is our great H** igh **P** riest

NEED TO KNOW

FILE FOUR

Endue

WHERE CAN I FIND IT?

This word can be found in the little book of James which is in the New Testament. It is the eighth book from the end of the New Testament and has just five chapters. In the third chapter, verse 13 contains the word ENDUE.

WHAT DOES IT MEAN?

The word ENDUE is very similar to the word ENDOW. It really means that something has been GRANTED TO or INVESTED IN a person. When this word ENDUE is used in the Bible it usually tells us about a person who has been GRANTED a special ability to be wise. In a sense God has INVESTED knowledge in them.

For extra info see CONCEPTS FILE 'T' for Talents

HOW CAN I USE IT?

God has INVESTED many things on our behalf. He INVESTED the blood of His Son to redeem us from our sins. He INVESTED the earth with water and air and the sun and moon for our benefit. He has INVESTED or

FILE FOUR continued

ENDUED each of us with many things which we use every day to learn, to work, to help others and to worship Him. These things are our TALENTS and we are held responsible for how we use them.

ASSIGNMENT [circle your answers]

■ JAMES is in the	NEW TESTAMENT	OLD TESTAMENT
◆ JAMES has 5 Chapters.	4 CHAPTERS	6 CHAPTERS
● ENDUE means	WITHHELD	GRANTED

THE F FILES

TOP SECRET

FILE ONE

Fain

WHERE CAN I FIND IT?

This little word can be found in a very famous story. If you go to the third gospel in the New Testament, Luke, and find chapter fifteen. In verse sixteen you will see the word FAIN.

WHAT DOES IT MEAN?

FAIN means GLADLY or WILLINGLY. But it is the sort of willingness to do something because there is no other choice. You may not like the taste of medicine but you GLADLY take it if you know it will make you stop barfing! Now, that isn't the same sort of gladness you feel when you eat something you really enjoy, is it? The word FAIN is the sort of gladness that comes from having no other choice.

HOW CAN I USE IT?

The famous story in which you found this verse was of course the story of the prodigal son (prodigal means wasteful or extravagant). When it turned out that the prodigal son had no money or no food left he would gladly have eaten the pigs dinner! We can all be wasteful and extravagant with the things which God has given to us, even everyday things like water. If we waste things we will end up having to do with much less. This little word FAIN is the sort of gladness which we never want to be constrained or forced to experience! No pig's dinner thank you very much, it's better not to be wasteful!

i There is a SPECIAL ASSIGNMENT on the next page

SPECIAL ASSIGNMENT

CLASSIFIED

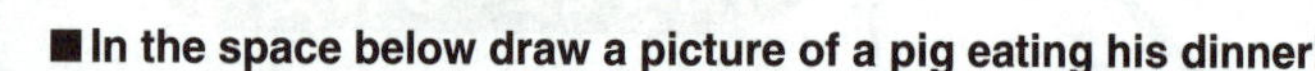

■ **In the space below draw a picture of a pig eating his dinner!**

◆ **Draw your favourite dinner on the dinner plate below!**

THE F FILES

NEED TO KNOW

FILE TWO

Fetters

WHERE CAN I FIND IT?

The book of Judges is in the Old Testament. In fact it is the seventh book and it has 21 chapters. Judges introduces us to the strong man Samson. In chapter sixteen of the book of Judges and in verse 21 you will find the word FETTERS.

WHAT DOES IT MEAN?

FETTERS were metal bands which were placed around a prisoner so that the person captured would not find it easy to escape. These bands usually had chains attached to them as well. They were heavy, deep cuffs which could be put on a prisoner's wrists and ankles, or even around their waist like a belt. FETTERS or SHACKLES as they are sometimes called were very painful. Much more so than the skinny wee handcuffs which are used today.

HOW CAN I USE IT?

Samson, as you know was Mr. Strong! He could lift a city gate and carry it on his shoulder! He could tie foxes together! He could kill a lion with his bare hands. So how come he wound up captured and made a prisoner with brass fetters fitted to his body? He told the secret of his strength to someone who turned out to be his enemy. When we replace good with bad, in a sense we too are letting ourselves have fetters fitted to us. Sins are heavy things, you know. They are uncomfortable and they don't suit

FILE TWO

continued

anybody. We are made in the image of God. That means we are made to be like God. Now, could you ever see God being bound up in fetters? I don't think so! He is far too wise. He cannot sin. Do you really want weighty cuffs and ankle bands and chains hanging around you all your life? Certainly not. Stick with the truth, do what is right and remember God won't let the Devil near you with his fetters of sin!

ASSIGNMENT [answers these questions]

■ **READ the story of Samson and find out how he became a WINNER in the end! THEN answer these questions.**

- ◆ **Did SAMSON'S hair grow again?** ....yes!....
- ● **The god of the Philistines was called** ....Dagon....
- ▲ **SAMSON was set between two** ....pillars....
- ● **How many men and women were on the roof?** ....3000....
- ◆ **How many years did Samson judge Israel?** ....20 years....

THE F FILES

TOP SECRET

FILE THREE

Foreknowledge

WHERE CAN I FIND IT?

This long word FOREKNOWLEDGE can be found in the New Testament book of Acts, in chapter two and verse 23.

WHAT DOES IT MEAN?

You and I are very much linked to time. We judge how long a job takes by time. We get up and go to bed according to time. Our lives are measured by time. God is not dominated or ruled by time the way we are. This word FOREKNOWLEDGE implies the ABSENCE OF TIME in the past, in the present, and in the future. You and I cannot possess FOREKNOWLEDGE. It is what we call an ATTRIBUTE of God. That means it is a CHARACTERISTIC of God. FOREKNOWLEDGE is something which makes God God. It makes Him supreme to us in the same way as His holiness or goodness does.

ASSIGNMENT ON NEXT PAGE

HOW CAN I USE IT?

If God knows all things then He knows all about the things which will happen to us. What's more He has things arranged in a plan for our lives. Now sometimes these are hard and difficult things for us to understand. Sometimes they are straightforward things which we don't wonder about at all. Sometimes they are things which bring a big smile to our faces! But

CLASSIFIED

FILE THREE

continued

God takes all of these things - like a big jigsaw puzzle which we can't make head nor tail of, and He fits them altogether, bit by bit, to create the life He wants for us. I don't know about you, but jigsaw puzzles aren't my thing at all! And, when I think about something as large and complicated as my life I'm mighty glad that it is God who is fitting it together and not me!

ASSIGNMENT [fill in the gaps]

■ God is not ruled by T ime

◆ FOREKNOWLEDGE is an A ttribute of God.

THE F FILES

NEED TO KNOW

FILE FOUR

Faith

WHERE CAN I FIND IT?

The first Gospel - Matthew, chapter eight verse ten has the word FAITH in it.

WHAT DOES IT MEAN?

FAITH is FIRM BELIEF or TRUST in a person, or in a thing, or in a statement. The FAITH which we read about in the Bible is about TRUST in Jesus Christ and BELIEF in His statements or words. These we read in the Bible. SAVING FAITH is the FAITH which leads us to accept Jesus as our Saviour. We believe He died for us and ask Him to save us from our sins.

HOW CAN I USE IT?

The first thing which FAITH does for us is that it justifies us. You can look up the word JUSTIFICATION in the concepts file to find out about this.
The second thing which FAITH does for us is that it produces in us love for God and love for our neighbours. Our neighbours aren't just the people who live next door to us, they are the people who we find next to, or beside us, throughout our lives.
There is another lovely thing which the word FAITH teaches us and that is that God Himself is FAITHFUL to us! God is full of trust when it comes to dealing with you and me. He never lies to us. He never cheats on us. He never is unkind or unjust to us. FAITHFULNESS is another ATTRIBUTE of God.

ASSIGNMENT [underline your answers]

■ Faith = T rust. Faith J ustifies me.

◆ Faithfulness is an A ttribute of God.

TOP SECRET

FILE ONE

Garner

WHERE CAN I FIND IT?

If you find Luke, which is the third of the four gospels, in chapter three verse 17 you will spot the word GARNER. Luke has 24 chapters making it the second biggest of the four gospels. Matthew has 28 chapters and is the longest. John has 21 chapters and Mark is the shortest with 16 chapters.

WHAT DOES IT MEAN?

A GARNER was a STORE FOR GRAIN or what we call a BARN nowadays. It is where the farmer puts the grain which he has gathered or harvested, so that it is not left outside where the wind and rain of winter would destroy it.

YOUR ASSIGNMENT IS ON THE NEXT PAGE

HOW CAN I USE IT?

Quite often in the Bible you will read stores about grain or wheat. The CHAFF is the part of the grain which has no nutritional value. It is the waste or the remains after the good grain has been separated. This process is called WINNOWING. The Bible tells us that people who don't consider God to be of any importance are like CHAFF. Such a person is

SECRET

FILE ONE

continued

UNGODLY and they have nothing of substance in their life. Like the husks of the grain they can be blown away by the wind. Those who love God and seek to obey Him are like the good part of the grain. They are kept safe in Jesus just as the valuable wheat is kept safe in the GARNER or barn.

ASSIGNMENT [answer these questions]

- **Can you find PSALM NUMBER ONE?**  **NO**

- **Now search out the word CHAFF and write which verse it is in** 

THE G FILES

TOP SECRET

FILE TWO

Glory

WHERE CAN I FIND IT?

My favourite chapter in the Bible is actually a Psalm. Do you have a favourite chapter or a favourite verse maybe? Anyway, this word GLORY can be found in verse one of the Psalm which I like very much. The Psalm is number 19. Can you find the word GLORY in the first verse?

WHAT DOES IT MEAN?

God's GLORY is displayed to us IN THE WORKS OF HIS CREATION. That is what the verse in Psalm 19 which you just found explains to us. In fact if you read some more verses you will see that the psalmist continues with this explanation about God's GLORY.

God's GLORY is also displayed to us in HIS PROVISION for us. Not just in His providing things which we need for survival on earth, but also in how He has provided for us the way to eternal life.

God's GLORY is why we worship Him. It makes us realise that He is all powerful and worthy or fit to be worshipped. GLORY is the EXCELLENCE of God.

YOUR ASSIGNMENT IS ON THE NEXT PAGE

HOW CAN I USE IT?

We are instructed in the Bible to give GLORY to God. We do this by exalting Him above everyone else and above everything else in our lives. God's GLORY is very precious to Him and He will not give it to any other

FILE TWO

continued

god. This is why we need to treat even the name of God with honour and respect as we are commanded to in the first and second commandments.

ASSIGNMENT [circle your answers]

- Can you find EXODUS chapter 20 and read these two commandments in verses 3,4,5 and 6?

  YES NO

- Can you find ISAIAH chapter 42 verse 8 and read about the word GLORY?

  YES NO

REMEMBER - THESE TWO BOOKS ARE BOTH IN THE OLD TESTAMENT

THE G FILES

CLASSIFIED

FILE THREE

Grafted

WHERE CAN I FIND IT?

In Romans chapter 11 verse 17 you will be able to find this word GRAFFED. As this verse is part of an illustration you might like to read the next verses as well. Verses 19, 23, 24 also have this word GRAFFED in them.

WHAT DOES IT MEAN?

GRAFFED really means the same as GRAFTED. To GRAFF or GRAFT is to take a shoot or bud of one tree and insert it into the branch of another. The bud which has been GRAFTED is usually better than the branch onto which it is GRAFTED. The result is that one tree may have two types of fruit growing on it.

HOW CAN I USE IT?

You and I can have God's love GRAFTED into our hearts when we accept Him as our Saviour. When we become part of His family His love produces good fruit in our lives.

ASSIGNMENT [fill in the gaps]

■ To find what these good fruits are look up GALATIANS chapter 5 verse 22 and 23. Why don't you list them below

Love	Longsuffering	Faith
Joy	Gentleness	Meckness
Peace	Goodness	Temperance

THE G FILES

NEED TO KNOW

FILE FOUR

Glistering

WHERE CAN I FIND IT?

There are two books in the Old Testament called Chronicles. First Chronicles has 29 chapters and Second Chronicles is a bit bigger with 36 chapters. This lovely word GLISTERING can be found in First Chronicles chapter 29 verse 2. This is quite a long verse so read it carefully to find this word.

WHAT DOES IT MEAN?

GLISTERING means SHINING. Now there is shine and there is shine! Some things which shine are brash and bright and hurtful to the eyes. But, some things which shine are really beautiful. When you read this word GLISTERING in the Bible it is the sort of shine which is beautiful.

HOW CAN I USE IT?

When Jesus went up into a mountain to pray with Peter, John and James the Bible tells us that as he prayed His appearance changed. It also says that His clothing was white and GLISTERING. The beauty of Jesus is a shining beauty. It is the most lovely GLISTERING we will ever see!

ASSIGNMENT [fill in the gaps]

■ **Luke 9 verse 29 has the word GLISTERING in it. If you read this chapter you will learn who Peter, James and John saw with Jesus when they prayed together in the mountain. Write their names below.**

E lias and M oses

Halt

WHERE CAN I FIND IT?

As this word has two meanings you can find it in two different verses. The first you will find in First Kings 18 verse 21. The second you will find in the gospel of Mark chapter nine verse 45. That is, one in the Old Testament and one in the New Testament!

WHAT DOES IT MEAN?

Let's look at the meaning in the verse which you found in First Kings. This is the meaning which you probably already knew for the word HALT. It simply means STOP. We may stop because we are instructed to do so or we may STOP because we are unsure what to do next. We may even STOP because we have finished.
Now let's put the word STOP into the verse in Mark which you found. If we replace HALT in this verse with STOP it doesn't really work, does it? The meaning of the word HALT here is actually LAME or CRIPPLED. If we use one of these words instead, we get the sense of what is being taught in this verse.

HOW CAN I USE IT?

There are two things offered to us every day of our lives. There is good and there is bad - right and wrong. Every day we make choices. Sometimes when a major decision or choice has to be made by us instead of at

SECRET

FILE ONE

continued

once choosing what is right - we HALT. We hesitate. We listen to the arguments in favour of the wrong choice. God prefers us not to even think about doing the wrong thing. That leaves us open to TEMPTATION and it means that the Devil is in with a chance of winning! So, when it comes to choosing between right and wrong - don't even think about HALTING, just do right!

ASSIGNMENT [fill in the box]

■ **There is a great story in LUKE chapter 14 in which the word HALT is used with its meaning of CRIPPLED. It is a story about a man who invited a stack of friends to his place for a big meal. Guess what? Nobody showed! See if you can find what he did and write below which verse the word HALT is in. The story begins at verse 16**

◆ **I found the word HALT in verse** 

NEED TO KNOW

FILE TWO

Hart

WHERE CAN I FIND IT?

Psalm 42 verse one probably is the best known place in the Bible where this word appears.

WHAT DOES IT MEAN?

The HART is one of the most graceful and beautiful animals which God has created. When it is tired and thirsty it pants the way a dog pants. Another name for the HART is the ROE or ROE-BUCK. Often you will read about the HART and the ROE in the Bible. Usually its ability to run swiftly and its elegance are the two things which are mentioned. The HART also is known for having beautiful eyes. It is a very affectionate yet timid animal. It is like a deer.

HOW CAN I USE IT?

The verse in Psalm 42 which you read and found the word HART in also tells us that the HART pants for water. This teaches us that we should read the Bible in the same sort of way that the HART pants for water. Now, of course it doesn't mean we sit and make a noise like a dog when we read the Bible! That would be daft altogether! It means that we should be eager or thirsty for the words which we read in the Bible and which teach us about God. Reading the Bible shouldn't be a hard thing to do. We should enjoy it and search for new words and new stories as we read. Just like the HART gets thirsty and longs for water, so we should look forward to a great big drink of words from the Bible every day!

ASSIGNMENT [fill in the gaps]

■ When I read the BIBLE I will be sure to E n j o y it!

TOP SECRET

FILE THREE

Heart

WHERE CAN I FIND IT?

In the Old Testament the book of Jeremiah comes after the book of Isaiah. This is easy to remember because they sort of rhyme - Isaiah, Jeremiah - don't they? In Jeremiah chapter 17 verse 10 you can find the word HEART.

WHAT DOES IT MEAN?

Well, you probably know what your HEART is. It is the muscle which acts as a pump to keep your body alive. It is important to exercise and eat good food so that this pump is in good working order! When you read the word HEART in the Bible it really means a good bit more of you than your actual HEART. Your ACTUAL HEART keeps you healthy. Your SPIRITUAL HEART keeps you good. It ensures you have healthy thoughts and a pure mind.

HOW CAN I USE IT?

The verse which you found in Jeremiah tells you that the Lord searches the HEART. Now, of course, He doesn't open up your chest and look at your heart the way a doctor may have to if you had a sick heart. But he does search your SPIRITUAL HEART to make sure there are no dirty SIN BUGS that might stop it pumping good thoughts into your mind.
We often say that we love someone with all our hearts. Just as we know that it is not our ACTUAL HEART which loves the person, so too do we understand that when we love the Lord Jesus with all our heart, we mean that all of our being loves Him.

SPECIAL ASSIGNMENT

CLASSIFIED

■ **Psalm 119 is very long indeed. It has 176 verses in it! If you find this Psalm, verse 11 has the word HEART in it. Why don't you find this verse then draw a big heart in the space below, and copy the words of the verse into the heart!**

Psalm 119V11

Thou puttest
away all the
wicked of the
earth like
dross:
therefore
I love
My
testimonies.

THE H FILES

TOP SECRET

FILE FOUR

Hosanna

WHERE CAN I FIND IT?

This unusual word can be found in Matthew chapter 21 verse nine. In fact, you will find it twice in this verse.

WHAT DOES IT MEAN?

This is a Hebrew word. That means it is taken from the Hebrew language in which the New Testament was originally written. That was the language of the day. The word HOSANNA means SAVE NOW or SAVE WE PRAY! and it was a shout of praise, a sort of greeting. This was the word which the people all shouted when Jesus rode into Jerusalem before He was crucified.

HOW CAN I USE IT?

Well, it wouldn't make much sense to people nowadays if you shouted HOSANNA at them! But, the word HOSANNA reminds us of the day Jesus rode into Jerusalem and the people cheered Him and cut down branches from the trees and threw these on the roadway to form a carpet. Someday Jesus will come back to this earth, as He promised He would, and the word HOSANNA will be a good word to greet Him with if we are alive when He returns!

ASSIGNMENT [which of these is the right meaning?]

- ■ HOSANNA is a FRENCH word which means HAPPY
- ◆ HOSANNA is a GREEK word which means BRANCH
- ● HOSANNA is a HEBREW word which means SAVE WE PRAY

THE | FILES

NEED TO KNOW

Image

WHERE CAN I FIND IT?

This word can be found in the second commandment, so turn to Exodus chapter 20 in your Bible and search for this word IMAGE in verse four.

WHAT DOES IT MEAN?

An IMAGE is a representation or likeness of a person or a thing. But in the second commandment God's rule about IMAGES is that they must not be worshipped. An IMAGE which man makes and then worships is an IDOL. If we worship an IMAGE instead of the true God this is called IDOLATRY. Idolatry is one of two things. It can be that instead of worshipping God a person worships some other person or thing that has been made, such as an IMAGE. Images are usually painted or carved statues or figures. Or, IDOLATRY can be that a person worships the true God under some image. These are things which people regard as emblems of God, but which are not God Himself. This is dangerous because the emblem can easily replace God and be worshipped instead of Him.

Do you know about the IMAGE which lost its head and hands? See I SAMUEL 5 verse 4

HOW CAN I USE IT?

The second commandment is important because God is our King and so IDOLATRY or using IMAGES to worship Him is really treason! Treason

CLASSIFIED

FILE ONE

continued

means we are being disloyal to our King. Nothing in our lives should ever replace God or be loved more by us than God. Because this matters to God, it must matter to us.

ASSIGNMENT [fill in the gaps]

■ **Can you find the type of IMAGE which the Children of Israel made in EXODUS chapter 32? (Try looking in verses 3 and 4!) When you find it can you fill in the gaps?**

◆ **Aaron made an IMAGE of a C**aLf**. It was made of G**old**.**

THE FILES

TOP SECRET

FILE TWO

Iniquity

WHERE CAN I FIND IT?

In Psalm number 32 verse five you will be able to find this word twice.

WHAT DOES IT MEAN?

INIQUITY is anything we do which is AGAINST GOD'S LAW or the rules which God has asked us to obey. When we sin, we BREAK God's law. When we commit INIQUITY we show CONTEMPT or DISREGARD for God's law. So as well as breaking God's law, we treat it as worthless. INIQUITY is a BAD ATTITUDE to God and His rules.

HOW CAN I USE IT?

In the verse which you found in Psalm 32 you will learn that God forgives not only our sin but also our INIQUITY. He forgives the things which we did wrong and the manner in which we did them. Sometimes it is easier to do something right than it is to do something in a gracious or kind way! God knows this and so He extends His goodness and love and forgiveness even further than we deserve. And, the result? Well, the result is that our bad attitude gets the forgiveness treatment too! That's pretty amazing, isn't it? In fact, it makes you want to have a good attitude!

ASSIGNMENT [circle the correct verse]

■ **You found the word INIQUITY two times in verse 5 of Psalm 32. Can you find it another time in verse 2? When you do, give yourself a big STAR in this box!**

THE | FILES CLASSIFIED

FILE THREE

Inheritance

WHERE CAN I FIND IT?

You know the book of Psalms very well now because you have searched for many words in it. This time find the 47th Psalm and find this rather long word INHERITANCE in verse four.

WHAT DOES IT MEAN?

An INHERITANCE is something which is left to you when a member of your family dies. You would receive it as an HEIR. This is why we call the son or daughter of a King or Queen the HEIR to the Throne. Their INHERITANCE will be to become King or Queen. An INHERITANCE may be several things. It may be money. It may be land or property. It may be a business or it may be valuable jewellery or even a valuable painting. An INHERITANCE therefore has an influence on your future.

HOW CAN I USE IT?

The verse which you searched for in Psalm 47 teaches that God has chosen our INHERITANCE for us. Now, if you look in the New Testament book of Matthew, the very first gospel, and find chapter 25 verse 34 you will find what you will INHERIT! You will INHERIT eternal life. Jesus died in order that we might be with Him in heaven when we die. This makes us HEIRS of the Kingdom of God along with Jesus His Son!

ASSIGNMENT

■ **Why don't you read this wonderful FACT for yourself in ROMANS chapter 8 verses 16,17. DON'T EVER FORGET IT NOW!**

THE FILES

NEED TO KNOW

Inspiration

WHERE CAN I FIND IT?

The second book of Timothy chapter three verse 16 has this big word in it. You might want to read verse 17 as well, as it finishes off the meaning and will help you to understand it better.

WHAT DOES IT MEAN?

God influenced the minds of the men who wrote the Bible so that what they wrote was what God wanted written. This process or method which God used is called INSPIRATION. It is this which makes the Bible a book of AUTHORITY. That means it has been SANCTIONED or APPROVED by God as the book which tells us the gospel and teaches us the commandments. It means the Bible is a very precious book.

HOW CAN I USE IT?

Let's look again at the verses in Timothy where you found the word INSPIRATION. They tell first of all that the Scripture or Bible is INSPIRED, which means it is a record of God's words to us. Then verse 16 tells us why these words are important. It gives four reasons:

1. The Bible contains **DOCTRINE** - that means it has God's rules in it.
2. The Bible contains **REPROOF** - that means it tells us what is wrong.

FILE FOUR

continued

3. The Bible contains **CORRECTION** - that means it teaches us to do right.
4. The Bible contains **INSTRUCTION** - that means it tells us wonderful things about God, about His Son, and about us as His children.

Then, verse 17 tells us why God wants us to read the Bible - so that we will have KNOWLEDGE of God and do GOOD.

ASSIGNMENT [fill in the gaps]

■ Can you list the four things which the INSPIRED Word of God contains?

Doctrine

Reproof

Correction

Instruction

THE J FILES

CLASSIFIED

FILE ONE

Jubile

WHERE CAN I FIND IT?

Leviticus is the third book of the Bible, so it is an easy book to find! It has 27 chapters in all but you need to find chapter 25 verse 9 in order to see the word JUBILE.

WHAT DOES IT MEAN?

The JUBILE or what nowadays we would call JUBILEE was an event which was celebrated by the Jews once every FIFTY YEARS. It began with the sound of the trumpet or horn - that is why you might hear the saying 'sound the jubilee'. You might also hear it said that someone is celebrating their golden jubilee. This means it marks 50 years of marriage or it could also refer to 50 years of a business or 50 years since an important event.

HOW CAN I USE IT?

The year of JUBILEE was an outstanding event or appointment of Jewish law. Once every fifty years some incredible things were permitted. All Hebrew servants were set free! Individuals, families and whole communities were restored or given back everything that was theirs 50 years earlier! Inheritances which had been transferred to another family were returned to the family to whom they had originally belonged! Because the effect of the year of jubilee was set in law, people were very careful in their business affairs and in how they dealt with others. They knew that if they did wrong, the year of Jubilee would simply take from them what ought not to have been theirs! This law meant that injustices and wrong-

doing was avoided in society. The JUBILEE year kept everything nice and fresh and well ordered in the Hebrew state. You and I know that one day we will die. Death is nothing that we should be afraid of because Jesus rose from the dead. In a way our death will be like our jubilee year. The inheritance of eternal life we have which the devil tries to take from us, will be given to us by God. Because we know this event is going to happen, just as the Hebrews knew the jubilee would happen, we should be careful to be well prepared to meet Jesus. Every day we need to confess our sins to Him and ask Him to help us do right. We should seek to be ACCEPTABLE or APPROVED by God.

ASSIGNMENT [can you find the right number?]

■ **The JUBILEE came along once every**

10 years	**25 years**	**40 years**
50 years	**500 years**	**1000 years**

THE J FILES

TOP SECRET

FILE TWO

Jangling

WHERE CAN I FIND IT?

You have found several words in the books called Timothy so it won't take you long to search for this funny word JANGLING. Look in the first book of Timothy chapter one verse 6.

WHAT DOES IT MEAN?

The word JANGLING always reminds me of bells. Tiny bells which jangle or make an annoying noise (now jingle bells are something much better, aren't they?). In the Bible this word JANGLING means FOOLISH TALK. It is the sort of talk which is vain or self-centred and it is the complete opposite of God's rule about charity or love for each other.

HOW CAN I USE IT?

JANGLING words not only annoy other people, but they upset God. When we are God's children we are all part of a big family and He is our Father. Another word for Father is ABBA. As our Father, God wishes us to be loyal and kind to one another within this special family. He also wants us to be honest and good to people who are not yet in His family, otherwise they will not want to become part of the family of God. After all, would you want to join a family that spoke only foolishness? I doubt it!

SPECIAL ASSIGNMENT

SECRET

■ **JANGLING words are F oolish words**

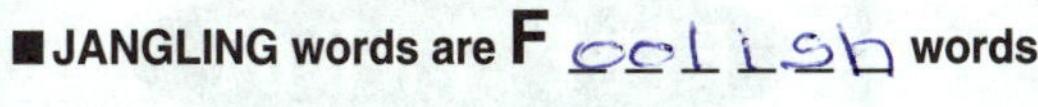

◆ **In the space below draw some silly wee bells that make an annoying noise. Then draw a nice big bell in your favourite colour and REMEMBER your words should always be lovely.**

THE J FILES

NEED TO KNOW

FILE THREE

Jot

WHERE CAN I FIND IT?

This is such a wee word, make sure you don't miss it when you look for it in Matthew chapter five verse 18.

WHAT DOES IT MEAN?

A JOT is the smallest letter in the Hebrew alphabet. It is a bit like the shape of our comma, so it is very small isn't it? There is another tiny mark used in Hebrew letters called a TITTLE - that's a funny one too, isn't it? Anyway, the JOT and the TITTLE are two tiny parts of the Hebrew language.

HOW CAN I USE IT?

The verse in which you found this wee word JOT also has the word TITTLE in it. I'm sure you noticed that. It explains to us that even the smallest or least of God's rules are important and won't be changed by Him as long as earth exists. The wee things are as important as the big things. If we get the small things right, it makes it easier to get the big things right too.

ASSIGNMENT

- Make a mark like a tiny JOT in this box 
- Make a mark like a tiny TITTLE in this box 
- Are the wee things as important as the big things?  YES NO

FILE FOUR

Jehovah

WHERE CAN I FIND IT?

Psalm number 83 verse 18 contains this big word JEHOVAH. In my Bible it is printed in nice big capital letters. Is it printed like that in yours?

WHAT DOES IT MEAN?

JEHOVAH is a title which belongs only to God. It reminds us that God doesn't need anybody else to help Him to exist. He is SELF-EXISTING.He is completely INDEPENDENT. He is completely RIGHT. He is ETERNAL. The word JEHOVAH sometimes has another word attached to it. Here are some examples which you might hear being used. In case you want to search for them, I shall include the verses where you can find them. This could be a special task for you to carry out!

JEHOVAH-JIREH	This means God will provide. He meets our needs.	Genesis 22 v 14
JEHOVAH-NISSI	This means God is our banner. We carry His Name.	Exodus 17 v 15
JEHOVAH-SHALOM	This means God is peace. He gives us contentment.	Judges 6 v 25
JEHOVAH-TSIDKENU	This means God our righteousness. He has taken away our sins.	Jeremiah 23 v 6

SECRET

FILE FOUR

continued

HOW CAN I USE IT?

JEHOVAH is the special title of God which only His children really know because only His children know how very much He has loved them. As a child of God we know His kindness, His forgiveness and His protection. So we call God JEHOVAH, our special name for Him.

ASSIGNMENT [matching up]

Which of these can you match? Draw a line to link the word to its meaning.

■ JEHOVAH-JIREH	GOD OUR PEACE
● JEHOVAH-NISSI	GOD OUR RIGHTEOUSNESS
▲ JEHOVAH-SHALOM	GOD OUR PROVIDER
◆ JEHOVAH-TSIDKENU	GOD OUR BANER

THE K FILES

TOP SECRET

FILE ONE

Kine

WHERE CAN I FIND IT?

Deuteronomy is book number five of the Bible. It has 34 chapters. In chapter seven, verse 13 you will find this word KINE. It is quite a long verse, so be sure and read all of it so as not to miss this word!

WHAT DOES IT MEAN?

KINE are COWS! That's nice and easy to learn, isn't it? There is a well-known story about KINE in Genesis. Perhaps you have heard it before. It is in chapter forty one and it is about the KINE or the COWS which Pharaoh dreamt about. The word KINE can be found FIVE TIMES in verses 1-4. Can you spot them? It can be spotted FOUR TIMES in verses 18-20 and it can be found again TWICE in verse 26 and 27. If you find all these you will have found KINE eleven times!

HOW CAN I USE IT?

Have you ever heard somebody being called a 'silly cow'? You probably have.The book of Amos is towards the end of the Old Testament. Amos, who was a prophet, called the proud and unkind rulers of Israel, 'cows'! These rulers had become like lazy, greedy, selfish cows! He warned them that if they did not clean up their act God would be extremely cross with them. Cows are very lovely animals. They have wonderful eyes and soft kindly faces. They provide us with delicious milk. Their milk is used for all

SPECIAL ASSIGNMENT ON NEXT PAGE

CLASSIFIED

FILE FOUR continued

kinds of things, but if a cow gets greedy and selfish it becomes lazy and fat. God wants us to be useful cows not silly cows!

ASSIGNMENT [drawing]

■ Draw a big fat lazy cow here

■ Draw a beautiful useful cow and a big pint of milk!

THE K FILES

NEED TO KNOW

FILE TWO

Kinsman

WHERE CAN I FIND IT?

The book of Ruth is one of the smallest books in the Old Testament. It has only four chapters. That is easy to remember - four letters in the word Ruth and four chapters in the book Ruth!
In chapter two, verse one you will find the word KINSMAN.

WHAT DOES IT MEAN?

A KINSMAN is a MALE RELATIVE. A KINSWOMAN is a FEMALE RELATIVE. Our KIN are our family and relatives. There is a saying 'kith and kin' which refers to our KINDRED.
The book of Ruth tells a lovely story about a KINSMAN named Boaz. Why don't you read this story. Maybe you could count how many times you find the word KINSMAN.

HOW CAN I USE IT?

If you look for the word KINSMAN again, this time in chapter three verse nine, you will learn about the unusual request Ruth made of Boaz. She asked him to spread his robe over her. This is exactly what we do when we ask Jesus to save us. We ask Him to cover us beneath His precious blood so that He might be our REDEEMER or our KINSMAN. As a result we become part of his family. He is our next of KIN. Is the Lord Jesus Christ your KINSMAN?

ASSIGNMENT [fill in the gaps]

■ When you read the story of Ruth why don't you write down the names of the main characters. The first one is easy!

R uth N aomi B oaz.

TOP SECRET

FILE THREE

Kite

WHERE CAN I FIND IT?

Leviticus chapter 11 verse 14 has the word KITE in it. It is a tiny word and it is in a very short verse, so you should find it really quickly.

WHAT DOES IT MEAN?

You probably have flown a KITE or know what a KITE looks like but in the Bible a KITE is a BIRD. So when you read this word you had better not mistake it for the sort of KITE we are used to nowadays! It was a bird similar to a vulture or a hawk.

HOW CAN I USE IT?

In the Bible, in the Old Testament, there were certain things which were not to be eaten because they were considered unclean. God did not want them to be eaten by man. In fact if you read the verses before and after the one where you found the word KITE, you will learn what these were. There is quite a list!
The laws which God made man obey were changed by Him in the New Testament. This was because man no longer had to make sacrifices to atone for his sin, Jesus had come and made the great sacrifice for our sins. Laws like the Ten Commandments, of course, remained the same. The KITE is just one wee example of something which was considered unclean, now being considered clean. It is rather like you and me. We

SECRET

FILE THREE

continued

were once dirty and sinful. Then Jesus, when we asked Him to, cleansed us and made us fit for Heaven! Now, I am presuming that you have asked Him to cleanse away your sins? I sure hope you have!

ASSIGNMENT [fill in the gaps]

■ There is a verse in First John chapter one which tells us about this cleansing. It is verse seven and especially the last part of it. Find it and fill in the words below.

The blood of

Jesus Christ

cleanseth us from

all sin

THE K FILES

NEED TO KNOW

FILE FOUR

Kiss

WHERE CAN I FIND IT?

Psalm number two, verse 12 starts with this word KISS. Do you see it? Read all of the verse now, not just the first word!

WHAT DOES IT MEAN?

A KISS really has three meanings or three uses. These are the same today as they were throughout the time the Bible was written.

1. A KISS can be a GREETING. Often people will kiss one another on the cheek as a way of saying hello or goodbye.

2. A KISS can be a sign of LOVE and AFFECTION. This is a more intimate type of KISS than the sort which is used to say hello. We would KISS someone we love on the lips, but we wouldn't KISS someone we hardly knew or didn't know at all like that.

3. A KISS can be an act of WORSHIP or HOMAGE. In some religions people will kiss a cross or a ring or even a statue. Some times they will kiss the object and then touch it on their forehead.

So, the type of KISS you give someone indicates what you mean by it.

HOW CAN I USE IT?

There is nothing at all wrong with kissing someone to greet them or with kissing someone you love, but God does not permit us to kiss another

FILE FOUR

continued

god nor another emblem of a god. In the verse which you found in Psalm two we are told to 'kiss the son'. This is God's way of underlining to us the importance of paying respect and giving worship to Him alone. He is the only God we can trust.

ASSIGNMENT

■ **Remember, the 10 Commandments teach us not to worship any other god except the true God. Find this Commandment in Exodus chapter 20 verse 3 and fill in the gaps below.**

It says: 'Thou shalt have no other gods before me'

This is the first **Commandment**

THE L FILES

TOP SECRET

FILE ONE

Lake

WHERE CAN I FIND IT?

Revelation is the last book in the Bible. It has 22 chapters. The chapter you want to locate is number 20, so it is almost at the very end of your Bible. Find verse 10 and search for this word LAKE.

WHAT DOES IT MEAN?

Usually when you would read the word LAKE in the Bible it means exactly the same as the word LAKE means to us today. LAKES are expanses of water which are inland, away from the sea. LAKES can be large or small. The main LAKES which you read about in the Bible are the LAKE TIBERIAS or GENNESARET; the SALT SEA or the DEAD SEA and the LAKE MEROM. There is another LAKE which you will have discovered when you found this word - it is the LAKE OF FIRE. This is the LAKE into which the Devil will be cast for ever and ever. There is also brimstone in this LAKE. (Remember brimstone from the B files? It is sulphur).

For extra info see CONCEPTS FILE H for Hell

HOW CAN I USE IT?

If you look at verse 15 of the same chapter, you can find the word LAKE again. This time we learn that whoever is not found written in the Book of Life will be cast into the LAKE of fire. When Jesus becomes our Saviour

He writes our name into the Book of Life. If your name is in that book, you will never be cast into the LAKE of fire. That's a great escape, isn't it!

ASSIGNMENT

■ **This assignment requires you to think very carefully and answer very honestly.**

● **Is your name written in the book of life?** **YES** ☑ **NO** ☐

NEED TO KNOW

FILE TWO

Laver

WHERE CAN I FIND IT?

Exodus has lots of unusual and interesting words in it. Besides, being the second book of the Bible it's really easy to find! So we will go to Exodus again to find this word LAVER. It can be found in verse 18 of chapter 30.

WHAT DOES IT MEAN?

A LAVER was a circular container used in the Tabernacle. (Don't forget TABERNACLE is in your CONCEPTS FILE). It was made of polished brass and it contained water so that the priests could wash their hands and feet in it.

HOW CAN I USE IT?

When you or I come to Jesus to talk to Him in prayer, the first thing we need to do is ask Him to make our hearts pure. This requires that we confess or tell Him of the wrong things we have done or considered doing. When Jesus sees we are sorry for our sins He is more than ready to forgive them. Once we have been forgiven we are then ready to worship Him and ask Him about the things we need His help with. You see, when Jesus becomes our Saviour He not only forgives us our sins there and then, but He goes on forgiving us our sins. Just as we need to wash

SECRET

FILE TWO continued

ourselves every day - sometimes more than once too! - so we need to ask Jesus to get rid of the dirty sins which have stuck to us every day. We don't need a big LAVER of water to do this - we just need Jesus.

ASSIGNMENT [fill in the gaps]

- ■ I am SAVED by the B lood of Jesus.
- ● W ater cannot wash away my sins.
- ▲ I C onfess my sins to Jesus.

THE L FILES

CLASSIFIED

Leaven

WHERE CAN I FIND IT?

Another very easy book to find is the book of Matthew! In chapter 13 verse 33 you will find the word LEAVEN.

WHAT DOES IT MEAN?

LEAVEN is what we would call YEAST. It is the ingredient which we use to make bread RISE and be LIGHT, otherwise bread would remain flat and be much more dense or heavy in its texture. Bread made without LEAVEN is called UN-LEAVENED bread. LEAVEN changes the dough mixture very noticeably.

HOW CAN I USE IT?

Well, I suppose you can use it to make yourself some bread! But that doesn't really answer the question properly for you. The best answer is to look at the way Jesus used the word LEAVEN to illustrate the silent yet amazing influence which the gospel has on our lives. Read the verse again. What Jesus is teaching is this fact - that just as a little LEAVEN or YEAST can change a whole loaf, when He comes into our hearts we become different altogether.

ASSIGNMENT [fill in the gaps]

- **This fact is described in 2 Corinthians chapter 5 verses 17 -18. When you search these verses out and read them you can write below what you become.**

I am a New **C**reature

THE L FILES

TOP SECRET

Leviathan

WHERE CAN I FIND IT?

This is some word isn't it? You can find it in Psalm 104 verse 26.

WHAT DOES IT MEAN?

This is the Hebrew name for a SEA MONSTER! This sea monster would have looked like what we know to be crocodiles. It was a monster which had enormous strength and was a really fast swimmer. It had a huge mouth with about 40 teeth in the top and about 38 teeth in the bottom. It was covered in a callous and scaly coat which a canon ball couldn't have dented. Its big belly was its weakest spot.

HOW CAN I USE IT?

When this SEA MONSTER or LEVIATHAN appears in the Bible it describes a creature of strength and one which could destroy many things. In the Psalm where you found LEVIATHAN we learn in the next verses (27-29) that even a big monster like LEVIATHAN depends upon God. If God didn't provide food for LEVIATHAN to eat, if He didn't regard this big brute and give him breath - then even LEVIATHAN would die! No matter how strong someone is, no matter how fit, how powerful, how wealthy, it is God who created them and it is He who decides what will happen to them. Now that is real power!

YOUR ASSIGNMENT IS ON THE NEXT PAGE

SECRET

FILE FOUR continued

ASSIGNMENT [write out the verse]

■ Psalm 8 verse 9 proclaims the excellency of our God. It says: **O LORD OUR LORD, HOW EXCELLENT IS THY NAME IN ALL THE EARTH!**

● Can you learn this verse and write it out in this box below in nice bright colours?

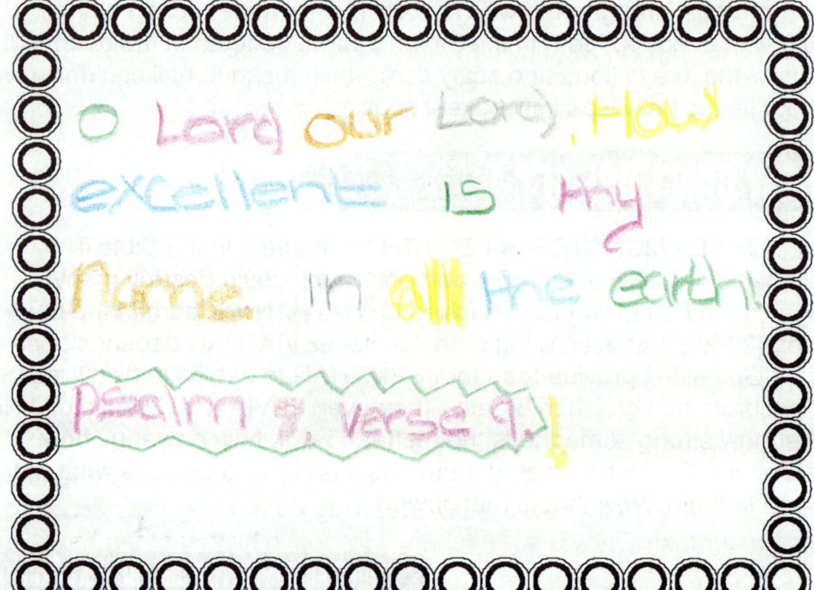

NEED TO KNOW

FILE ONE

Miracle

WHERE CAN I FIND IT?

You can find the word MIRACLE in the book of Acts chapter four and verse 22. Remember Acts comes immediately after the four gospels in the New Testament.

WHAT DOES IT MEAN?

A MIRACLE is a work which is beyond mankind's ability to perform. Any person who performs a miracle does it because God gives that person the power needed to cause a MIRACLE to happen. If God gives anyone this power it is for a great and extraordinary reason.

God gave some men, for example, His disciples, the power to work miracles in order to convince the world that they were speaking the truth. You will find MIRACLES in the Old Testament and MIRACLES in the New Testament. Of course the best known of all MIRACLES are the ones which we are told Jesus Himself performed when He was on earth.

HOW CAN I USE IT?

The age or time when MIRACLES are performed has gone but the record of them remains, so that we are still taught by them today. They confirm or reinforce our faith. They are evidence recorded in history of the heavenly

continued

nature of our religion. Our own salvation is the greatest miracle which Jesus has performed for us.

Before He saved us we were lost. Now we are found! We are going to Heaven and we are dressed in His very own righteousness.

For extra info see CONCEPTS FILE R for Righteousness

ASSIGNMENT [location test]

■ **Jesus peformed many miracles when He lived on earth. Some of them are recorded in the Bible. Find two of the five here and write down which ones you have found.**

THE MIRACLE	WHERE IT HAPPENED	RECORD OF IT
water into wine	Cana	John 2 vs 1-11
tempest calmed	Sea of Galilee	Matthew 8 vs 23-27
5000 fed	Decapolis	Matthew 14 vs 15-21
10 lepers cleansed	Samaria	Luke 17 vs 11-19
Malchus' ear healed	Gethsemane	Luke 22 vs 50-51

1) 10 lepers cleansed.

2) Malchus' ear healed

THE M FILES

CLASSIFIED

FILE TWO

Messias

WHERE CAN I FIND IT?

You can find this word in John chapter one verse 41. If you are smart you will see for whom it is another name.

WHAT DOES IT MEAN?

MESSIAS is the same name as MESSIAH. We probably know the word MESSIAH better. MESSIAH is a HEBREW word. It means ANOINTED ONE. MESSIAS is a GREEK word and means THE CHRIST.

The Old Testament was written in HEBREW and the New Testament in GREEK

HOW CAN I USE IT?

The MESSIAH, or CHRIST, is our prophet, our priest and our king. He is everything that was promised to us by God. This name or title for the Lord Jesus Christ reminds us of all the offices He holds. Just as we were promised a MESSIAH and the promise was fulfilled, or given, to us, so too we have been promised eternal life. And we will surely be given that as well.

ASSIGNMENT [location test]

- **To know for sure that you have eternal life find the PROMISE in John chapter 3 verse 16**

- **Tick this box if you found the promise** ☑

THE M FILES

TOP SECRET

FILE THREE

Mandrakes

WHERE CAN I FIND IT?

This is rather a strange word, and can be found in the book called The Song of Solomon which is in the Old Testament. It is three books after the book of Psalms and it has eight chapters. Find MANDRAKES in chapter seven verse 13.

WHAT DOES IT MEAN?

MANDRAKES were plants which emitted a very strong smell. The word is sometimes translated as a LOVE PLANT. Another plant called the MAY APPLE is sometimes used for the word MANDRAKE.

HOW CAN I USE IT?

MANDRAKES in the Bible are used in connection with lovers. The best gift which we can give to the Lord Jesus who loved us so much is the gift of our bodies. If we give ourselves completely to God He will help us to make the right choices throughout our lives.

ASSIGNMENT [fill in the gaps]

■ **Find ROMANS chapter 12 verse 1-2 and learn how important it is to give our bodies to God. Then fill in the gaps in this sentence.**

The greatest gift of my love to God is my Body.

THE M FILES

SECRET

FILE FOUR

Martyr

WHERE CAN I FIND IT?

In the book of Acts chapter 22 verse 20 this word can be found. Look also for the name of the MARTYR in this verse.

WHAT DOES IT MEAN?

A MARTYR is a person who is PUT TO DEATH for their BELIEFS. There have been many people throughout history who have been killed because they believed in God and would not deny Him or pretend not to love Him.

HOW CAN I USE IT?

As Christians we owe a great debt to people in history who refused to let the gospel story go untold. Their determination to love God, no matter what wicked men did to them, means that today we are free to worship God. These MARTYRS did not even fear death because they knew Jesus had overcome death and they would be with Him after their own death. The Bible teaches us that the only person we should fear is God, because He alone is all powerful. Men can only destroy our bodies. They can never ever destroy our souls or take away our eternal life in Heaven.

ASSIGNMENT [location test/circle your answer]

■ **This great fact is written in MATTHEW 10 verse 28. Read it for yourself.**

● **Who must we not fear?** **MAN** **GOD**

◆ **Who must we fear?** **GOD** **MAN**

THE N FILES

CLASSIFIED

FILE ONE

Naughtiness

WHERE CAN I FIND IT?

Proverbs, as you know, is a book of sayings. These sayings have important principles written into them. They give us good guidelines for how we live and think. Mostly, these sayings are easy to recall because they are written briefly and very much to the point! In other words they are 'short and sweet'.

In Proverbs chapter 11 verse 6 you will find the word NAUGHTINESS.

WHAT DOES IT MEAN?

Naughtiness in the Bible means something a bit like NAUGHTINESS as we think of it, only it is worse! If you are told you are being naughty, or to stop your naughtiness you are probably being badly behaved and you can correct it. But NAUGHTINESS in the Bible is extremely bad. It is sheer WICKEDNESS. It hurts others and traps the person who is being naughty too.

HOW CAN I USE IT?

We are told that NAUGHTINESS is something which we should put to one side. That means we should put it away from us. We can read this instruction in the book of James chapter one verse 21. James, unlike Proverbs, is in the New Testament. To understand fully what James is saying you should read verses 19 and 20 as well, and also verse 22 which tells you what you should be instead of naughty!

ASSIGNMENT [fill in the gaps]

■ **James tells us that we should be D**oers **of the W**ord.

THE N FILES

TOP SECRET

FILE TWO

Noised

WHERE CAN I FIND IT?

The book of Joshua isn't too far into the Old Testament. In fact, it is the fifth book and it has 24 chapters. In chapter six verse 27 you will see this word NOISED.

WHAT DOES IT MEAN?

The word NOISED means that something was TALKED ABOUT or WIDELY REPORTED. Today, we don't use the word noisy in quite the same way but I hope you agree that this is a lovely use of the word. People were in fact being noisy about something unusual. In this case it was Joshua's leadership. Later on in the New Testament it was used about miracles.

HOW CAN I USE IT?

We should be NOISY about the good things God gives to us - especially our salvation. Now, that doesn't mean that you go about yelling into people's ears! But, in the way the word is used in the Bible we should talk about Jesus to our friends. Jesus is never ashamed of us. He didn't come to earth to whisper to one or two people that He was the Messiah! We'd never have had a chance of Heaven if Jesus had acted ashamed of us. He let it be known by not only His words, but by His actions, that He loved us.

ASSIGNMENT [location test]

■ **PSALM 81 verse 1 tells us what sort of a noise we should be making. Why don't you read it and find out!**

THE N FILES

NEED TO KNOW

FILE THREE

Nether

WHERE CAN I FIND IT?

Ezekiel, in the Old Testament, is quite a big book with 48 chapters. You will need to search for chapter 31 verse 18 to find this word NETHER.

WHAT DOES IT MEAN?

NETHER means LOWER or BENEATH. It is easy to see this meaning in the verse where you found this word.

HOW CAN I USE IT?

When God is displeased with wickedness the people who are being wicked are separated from God. Our sins separated us from God. Jesus came and stood in the space between us and God. In a sense our sins put us into the NETHER parts of the earth. They put us so low that it took something as amazing as salvation to lift us up and make us approved by God.

ASSIGNMENT [circle your answer]

■ NETHER means	HIGHER	LOWER
● Who stands in the space between you and God?	JESUS	MARY
◆ How many chapters has Ezekiel?	31	48

THE N FILES

SECRET

FILE FOUR

Noisome

WHERE CAN I FIND IT?

Psalm 91 verse three has this word NOISOME in it. It is near the end of the verse so read it all!

WHAT DOES IT MEAN?

NOISOME sounds a bit like the word NOISED which we learned about earlier, but here NOISOME doesn't mean anything about sound. It means HURTFUL or even DEADLY!

HOW CAN I USE IT?

In this ninety-first Psalm we are being taught all about the safety which we have with God. As humans we are frail beings. We couldn't exist without God. As humans we become afraid by things which occur. We couldn't survive these without God. This Psalm reminds us that God is able to take away from us even the effects of deadly plagues!

ASSIGNMENT [memory test]

■ **Psalm 91 is a good Psalm to read when we need reminding of God's care for us. It reminds us that He even gives us a guardian angel to keep us safe. This is in verse 11. Maybe you could learn this lovely verse and ask someone to test you to make sure you know it.**

THE O FILES

TOP SECRET

FILE ONE

Oath

WHERE CAN I FIND IT?

This wee word with a very serious meaning can be looked for and found in James chapter 5 verse 12.

WHAT DOES IT MEAN?

To take an OATH means that you call on God to WITNESS or LISTEN to what you affirm or promise. If what you promise is not true or if you fail to do what you promise then God is most displeased. An OATH is a very serious thing indeed.

HOW CAN I USE IT?

OATHS should not be taken lightly by us. We should not take an OATH before any god other than the true God. We shouldn't take an OATH deceitfully. That means we cannot say one thing but really intend to do something else. We shouldn't take an OATH falsely, which means we mustn't lie when we take an OATH. And we must not rashly decide to take an OATH. This means we should never rush into making an OATH. We need to carefully consider everything that the promise says.

ASSIGNMENT [tick the boxes]

There are four main things we need to remember about OATHS. Tick the box beside the correct facts.

- [x] **Oaths may only be taken before the true God**
- [ ] **Oaths are funny**
- [x] **Oaths must not be deceitful**
- [ ] **Oaths can be broken because they don't matter**
- [ ] **Oaths do not need to be true**
- [x] **Oaths must not be false**

THE O FILES

CLASSIFIED

FILE TWO

Oracle

WHERE CAN I FIND IT?

In the second book of Samuel chapter 16 verse 23 the word ORACLE can be found.

WHAT DOES IT MEAN?

An ORACLE or ORACLES are sacred writings for us, the Bible. It is the WORD or the special writings which God has given to us.
Sometimes in the Bible the word ORACLE is used to describe the HOLY PLACE or TEMPLE where God revealed His will to ancient Israel.

HOW CAN I USE IT?

God's word or ORACLE is His message to us. That message not only leads us to believe or trust in Him, but it also helps us not to commit sin. It replaces the evil in our hearts with His love and with good desires. Knowing God's Word is important. If we don't know what God is telling us in His Word, we won't get to know Him at all.

ASSIGNMENT

■ **In Psalm 119 verse 11 you can learn this fact about God's Word keeping us from sin. Remember Psalm 119 is the longest of all Psalms but verse 11 is quite small. When you find it and read it, count how many words are in the verse and write the answer in the circle.**

THE O FILES

NEED TO KNOW

FILE THREE

Ouches

WHERE CAN I FIND IT?

Exodus chapter 39 verse six has the word OUCHES in it.

WHAT DOES IT MEAN?

When you or I use the word OUCH! we usually have been nipped by somebody or maybe stung! It's the sort of word we use if something gives us a jab of pain. But that meaning wouldn't really work in this verse, would it? No. OUCHES were special SOCKETS or HOLDERS for fastening precious stones onto the shoulder pieces of the High Priest's ephod - remember this word ephod from the E FILES?

HOW CAN I USE IT?

These OUCHES also worked a bit like buttons to hold in place the gold chains from which the High Priest's breastplate hung.
In a way we are like OUCHES or sockets. Just as these contained precious stones, so we have in us the precious Holy Spirit. The Holy Spirit is the presence of Jesus in our lives. This is a much more valuable thing than even the most expensive jewel!

ASSIGNMENT [circle your answers]

■ **Pick out the THREE PERSONS in the GODHEAD.**

THE MOTHER   THE FATHER   SAINT PAUL

THE SON   PETER   THE HOLY SPIRIT

THE O FILES

TOP SECRET

FILE FOUR

Ordinances

WHERE CAN I FIND IT?

This is quite a long word. You can find it easily enough in Exodus chapter 18 verse 20 because you know exactly where the book of Exodus is by now!

WHAT DOES IT MEAN?

An ORDINANCE is an ESTABLISHED LAW or RULE of God's GOVERNMENT. Government is how a country is run. Good government ensures that people's needs are met. Needs like clean water, proper housing and enough jobs to employ everyone. Good government provides schools and hospitals. Bad government allows these basic things to become shabby.

HOW CAN I USE IT?

God's ORDINANCES exist to keep our lives from becoming shabby. They are necessary for our well-being. The best thing for us to do is to obey them! We trust God for salvation and we obey Him for satisfaction.

ASSIGNMENT [circle your answers]

■ **Two key things which we do to have happy and well governed lives are in a hymn you might sing at Church or Sunday School. See if you can spot them.**

READ & PLAY **RUST & DECAY** **TRUST & OBEY**

SECRET

FILE ONE

Paradise

WHERE CAN I FIND IT?

In the third gospel of the New Testament, the book of Luke, you will find this beautiful word PARADISE. Look for it in chapter 23 verse 43.

WHAT DOES IT MEAN?

This word comes originally from Persia. It means a GARDEN or an ENCLOSED PLACE filled with beautiful scents and odours from the plants growing there. Sometimes the word is replaced with the word FOREST and sometimes with the word ORCHARD. So, the word PARADISE really conveys to us a place of beauty and happiness.

For extra INFO see CONCEPTS FILE H Heaven

HOW CAN I USE IT?

In the verse where you found the word PARADISE Jesus told the man who was on one of the crosses next to His that he would be with Him in PARADISE. This man realised that Jesus was the Son of God because he called Him 'Lord'. He also asked Jesus to 'remember him' and what an amazing answer he was given by Jesus! That very day, he would be with Jesus in PARADISE. The beautiful place of PARADISE can only be inhabited by redeemed human spirits.

SPECIAL ASSIGNMENT OVER PAGE

SPECIAL ASSIGNMENT

CLASSIFIED

■ **Draw a picture of what you think the place called PARADISE looks like. Won't it be great to see Jesus there?**

NEED TO KNOW

FILE TWO

Pardon

WHERE CAN I FIND IT?

Psalm number 25 verse 11 has the word PARDON in it. You will also see that it has the word INIQUITY in it. Can you recall what INIQUITY means? It is in the 'I' FILES.

WHAT DOES IT MEAN?

PARDON is really the COVERING of SIN or the BLOTTING OUT of our sin. The blood of Jesus is of course the only thing that can do this. God overlooks our sin because He sees instead the covering of the blood of His Son.

HOW CAN I USE IT?

When God PARDONS our sin He covers it so deeply that it is not possible to measure just how deep that is! He puts our sin so far, far away that He remembers it no more forever! God alone has the power to pardon and it is a result of the gift of salvation. Preachers, pastors, ministers and missionaries are commissioned, or given the job by God, to preach PARDON and salvation through the blood of Christ but no man can forgive sin or pretend that he has the right or ability to do so.

ASSIGNMENT [location test/circle your answer]

■ **Find Psalm 103 verse 12. Here you will find how far God puts our sin when He PARDONS us! He puts our sins as far as**

THE SOUTH IS FROM THE NORTH

THE EAST IS FROM THE WEST

TOP SECRET

Passion

WHERE CAN I FIND IT?

Acts chapter one verse three has the word PASSION in it. You know that Acts is the book which comes right after the four gospels. Can you remember what the next book is? It begins with the letter R.

WHAT DOES IT MEAN?

In the Bible the word PASSION has a special meaning as it refers to the LAST SUFFERINGS of Jesus Christ when He was on earth. The death of Jesus was the completion of His suffering.

HOW CAN I USE IT?

The PASSION of Christ reminds us of all that Jesus underwent in order to secure salvation for us. His PASSION or SUFFERING was taken willingly by Him. The Bible tells us that Jesus went to the cross with the attitude of a little lamb. A lamb is a gentle, beautiful little animal. As easily as a big cruel man could take a tiny wee lamb and kill it, so Jesus was taken by wicked men and hung on the cross. What a Saviour Jesus is!

ASSIGNMENT [memory test]

■ **Here is a verse of a hymn which tells us about the PASSION of Christ. Perhaps you could learn it as a reminder of what Jesus did for you. It also has the word PARDON in it.**

Bearing shame and scoffing rude,
In my place condemned He stood,
Sealed my pardon with His blood,
Hallelujah, what a Saviour!

THE P FILES

SECRET

FILE FOUR

Patriarch

WHERE CAN I FIND IT?

You found the last word, PASSION, in the book of Acts. Well, you can find this unusual word in that book as well. This time look in chapter two verse 29.

WHAT DOES IT MEAN?

A PATRIARCH is a FATHER FIGURE. In Bible times the PATRIARCH was the father of more than just a family, he was the leader of a race or a clan. When the father died, the eldest son usually became the PATRIARCH and the authority of the father was passed on to him.

HOW CAN I USE IT?

God is the PATRIARCH of our family. If we are children of God, He is our Father and we accept His authority. God is also the PATRIARCH of the Church. He is the head of the Church. No earthly person can be the head of the Church. This is God's place and He considers His Church to be His family.

ASSIGNMENT [circle your answers]

- Who is our PATRIARCH? JACOB MOSES  GOD
- Who is the Head of the Church? A POPE GOD A QUEEN
- Who is our Heavenly Father? GOD ST. JOHN PETER

THE Q FILES

NEED TO KNOW

FILE ONE

Quails

WHERE CAN I FIND IT?

In Exodus chapter 16 verse 13 you will find this funny wee word QUAIL.

WHAT DOES IT MEAN?

QUAILS were part of the food which God miraculously supplied for the children of Israel when they were in the wilderness. QUAILS are SMALL BIRDS and today they still can be found in the Mediterranean coasts and around the Red Sea.

HOW CAN I USE IT?

The other food which you probably have heard about was Manna. The story about QUAILS and Manna can be read in the same chapter in which you found the word QUAILS. This story shows the thoughtfulness of God and tells how He provides the things which we need - like food and water. We must never ever neglect to thank God for His goodness in giving these things to us.

ASSIGNMENT [location test]

- **The children of Israel were given QUAILS to eat on another occasion. You can find the story in the book of Numbers which comes right after Exodus. Look in chapter 11 and try finding the word QUAIL in verses 31-32.**

THE Q FILES

CLASSIFIED

FILE TWO

Queen

WHERE CAN I FIND IT?

If you find the book of Jeremiah in the Old Testament you will be able to see the word QUEEN in chapter seven verse 18.

WHAT DOES IT MEAN?

You probably are familiar with the word QUEEN. In our country, the United Kingdom, we have a QUEEN as our FIGUREHEAD. That means she is the person who represents our country. She doesn't rule our country, Parliament does that. In some countries the QUEEN (or King) still rules as well as being a figurehead. In the Bible the word QUEEN is also used to describe a false god - the QUEEN OF HEAVEN. This was the title given to the Moon by the people who worshipped it and not God.

HOW CAN I USE IT?

Remember, the first commandment teaches us that we are not to worship any gods except the true God. Well, the worship of the moon or the QUEEN OF HEAVEN is an example of how some people disobeyed this commandment. These people also broke the second commandment as well. It teaches us that we are not to make images to worship. These people made little cakes with the image of the moon on them and set up altars on the roofs of their houses and drank toasts to the QUEEN OF HEAVEN. All this to worship the moon! There is no such a person as the QUEEN OF HEAVEN. Heaven has a King and that King is God.

ASSIGNMENT [circle your answer]

■ **Which Commandments did the people break? 1 & 3 1 & 2 2 & 3**

THE Q FILES

TOP SECRET

FILE THREE

Quiver

WHERE CAN I FIND IT?

The book of Lamentations is in the Old Testament. It has only five chapters, making it one of the smallest books. It is the sixth book after the book of Psalms. If you find chapter three verse 13 you will find the word QUIVER.

WHAT DOES IT MEAN?

When we use the word QUIVER we usually mean quake or shake or shiver, but here the word QUIVER is the name given to a BOX or CASE used for keeping arrows in. Bows and arrows were very common in Bible times. Not only did men use them in war but they also used them to protect themselves and their flocks from wild animals. They also used them to hunt for food.

HOW CAN I USE IT?

A QUIVER was a SAFE PLACE to keep arrows in. They were stored there so as they would not be lost. In a way this is just how God looks after us. He keeps us hidden in Him. That means we are looked after and protected by God just as a QUIVER keeps arrows safe and secure.

ASSIGNMENT [LOOK ON NEXT PAGE FOR SPECIAL TASK]

■ **If you find Isaiah chapter 49 verse 2 you will read exactly this! Can you search for the word QUIVER in this long verse and fill in the gaps below?**

In his q uiver hath he h id me.

SPECIAL ASSIGNMENT

SECRET

■ **Draw your design for a QUIVER.**

A Quiver

THE Q FILES

NEED TO KNOW

FILE FOUR

Quicksands

WHERE CAN I FIND IT?

You know the book of Acts very well by now. You have searched for many words in it, so you should be quick at finding the word QUICKSANDS! Search in chapter 27 verse 17.

WHAT DOES IT MEAN?

QUICKSANDS are SHIFTING SANDS. They are dangerous and very powerful. They can swallow up people and animals and can cause currents so strong in the water that ships may be drawn or pulled off course.

HOW CAN I USE IT?

Our sins are just like QUICKSANDS. They pull us off course from doing right. They suck us in! QUICKSANDS are always moving position. Sin is like this. It is unsafe and unsure and nothing lasting can be built on the basis of our sin or wrong doing. Just like QUICKSANDS, sin is dangerous to us and will destroy us. Never forget how much danger you are in when you disobey God's laws.

ASSIGNMENT [reading]

■ **Find Matthew chapter 7 vs 24-27 and read a parable or story which Jesus told about a man who built his house on sand. It wasn't QUICK-SAND but it was just as unsafe.**

THE R FILES

TOP SECRET

FILE ONE

Redeem

WHERE CAN I FIND IT?

How would you like to find this word three times but only search out one verse? That sounds OK doesn't it? Three for the price of one! Search out Exodus chapter 13 and verse 13 to find the word REDEEM three times.

WHAT DOES IT MEAN?

To REDEEM a person is to BUY or PURCHASE their liberty. Liberty means freedom. The price which is paid is called the RANSOM. The Lord Jesus Christ gave His life for us. We are sinners and are in bondage to sin. Bondage means we are captured or held like a slave. We are controlled by sin. The blood which Jesus shed on the cross became our ransom. It was the price He paid to REDEEM us. But He only becomes our REDEEMER if we acknowledge Him as Lord. We must accept and believe that He died to save us.

HOW CAN I USE IT?

Well, first of all you need to make sure that you are REDEEMED! Then there is another way in which you can use the word REDEEM. You can REDEEM the time! This means that your life is very precious and so you must use your time with care. You ought not to waste time but take every opportunity that comes your way to do good.

ASSIGNMENT [location test]

■ **Find EPHESIANS 5 verse 16 to see this other use for the word REDEEM. Then turn over the page for another SPECIAL ASSIGNMENT.**

SPECIAL ASSIGNMENT

SECRET

■ **Fill in the missing words from the verse you looked up. Then, fill in the numbers on the clock below. Ask your Mum at what time you were born and fix the hands of the clock to that time as a reminder that your life is very precious.**

R edeem **the T** ime.

Ephesians 5 v 16

THE R FILES

NEED TO KNOW

FILE TWO

Reprobate

WHERE CAN I FIND IT?

This long and unusual word can be found in Jeremiah chapter six verse 30.

WHAT DOES IT MEAN?

REPROBATE is almost the same word as CASTAWAY or REJECTED. A person may be 'REPROBATE concerning the faith'. This can be read if you search for it in 2 Timothy chapter 3 verse 8. It means that they are FALSE BELIEVERS. A person may also be REPROBATE concerning their good works. Their good works are like false coins. They have no value because works cannot redeem or save.

HOW CAN I USE IT?

A REPROBATE is somebody you want nothing to do with! REPROBATES will water-down and weaken the words of the Bible and the laws of God until they are of no value at all. Would you prefer a bowl of soap suds or a bowl of lovely soup? Now, the soap suds might look pretty enough in a nice fancy soup bowl, but you'd soon see how rotten they were if you had to eat them! REPROBATES often look the part and act the part but when they are tested they don't half stink!

ASSIGNMENT [tick the box]

■ **Which of these R words would you rather be**

❑ **REPROBATE** ❑ **REDEEMED**

CLASSIFIED

FILE THREE

Rudiments

WHERE CAN I FIND IT?

This word can be found twice in the same chapter so why don't you search for it first of all in verse 8 and then in verse 20 of Colossians chapter two. Colossians is in the New Testament. It is the twelfth book.

WHAT DOES IT MEAN?

RUDIMENTS are BASIC or LOWEST principles. For example, you could say the RUDIMENTS of a language are found in its alphabet. RUDIMENTARY knowledge of something is a BASIC knowledge of the subject.

HOW CAN I USE IT?

In the verses where you found the word RUDIMENTS we are being taught that our basic principles as children of God are not the same as those who do not love Him. Our fundamental or basic principles must be founded on the Word of God, not on the world's values. The FUNDAMENTALS of our faith are very important and we should always remember what they are.

ASSIGNMENT [memory test]

■ **To remind you of the fundamentals of your faith there is a list of them on the next page. You can write them out again to help you learn them.**

TOP SECRET

FILE THREE

continued

1. The Bible is the Word of God
2. Jesus was born of a virgin
3. Jesus is my prophet, priest and king
4. Jesus shed His blood to pay for my sin
5. Jesus rose from the dead
6. Jesus is coming again

NOW - WRITE THEM DOWN!

1) The bible is the word of God

2) jesus was born of a virgin

3) jesus is my prophet, priest and king.

4) jesus shed his blood to pay for my sins.

5) jesus rose from the dead.

6) jesus is coming again

WELL DONE!

NEED TO KNOW

FILE FOUR

Rock

WHERE CAN I FIND IT?

This is a nice simple word to find. You know the book of Psalms very well now. So look for the word ROCK in Psalm 62. It is in verse two but if you read verse 1 as well you will have a better understanding of what the Psalmist is writing.

WHAT DOES IT MEAN?

You know the meaning of the word ROCK already, I'm sure. Rocks are very HARD and very STRONG. You could build a house on a ROCK! The word ROCK is used many times in the Bible to help us to understand how safe we are if we rust in God. You can find this word again if you search this time in the New Testament. Find the first book of Corinthians, chapter 10 verse 4. Here you will see this time the Bible is teaching us that Christ is our ROCK.

HOW CAN I USE IT?

There is no person, alive or dead, who can ever be our ROCK in the way which Christ can be. We are SAFE in Him alone. He is our hiding place and our protector. He is the ROCK of our salvation!

ASSIGNMENT [memorise this verse]

Jesus is the rock of my salvation and His banner over me is love.
Jesus is the rock of my salvation and His banner over me is love.
Jesus is the rock of my salvation and His banner over me is love.
His banner over me is love!

THE S FILES

CLASSIFIED

FILE ONE

Schism

WHERE CAN I FIND IT?

Isn't this an odd word!
You can find it in the first book of Corinthians chapter 12 verse 25.

WHAT DOES IT MEAN?

A SCHISM means a RUPTURE. A rupture is something which breaks apart or separates itself from the whole piece to which it belongs. Sometimes a person can have a part of their body RUPTURED. That means it is damaged and needs healed.
In the Bible this word is especially used to explain to us that the church, or the body of people who make up the church, should not be RUPTURED or separated from one another.

HOW CAN I USE IT?

We are all members of the family of God. In a way we are like a body. Just as each part of your body can do different things, so each of us can do different things to serve God. But God does not like us to hold any nasty feelings against another child of His. This creates a SCHISM or a rupture in the family of God. Whoever causes this SCHISM is the one who is doing wrong. If we cause separation between other believers we are sinning against God's love and we are disobeying His instruction about SCHISMS which you read when you searched for this word. If we love one another we are obeying God and won't be responsible for any awful ruptures!

SECRET

FILE ONE

continued

ASSIGNMENT [location/memory test]

■ Can you find the book of Romans chapter 13 verse 8? This tells us to love one another. Can you finish the verse below?

'... he that loveth another hath fulfilled the LAW.'

THE S FILES

NEED TO KNOW

FILE TWO

Scourge

WHERE CAN I FIND IT?

Which is the fourth Gospel? The answer is John. In John chapter 2 verse 15 you will find this word SCOURGE. In fact if you like, you could read verses 12 through to 22. This tells you about a SCOURGE which Jesus made.

WHAT DOES IT MEAN?

A SCOURGE was made of THREE CORDS or thongs of LEATHER bound together. One stroke equalled three lashes. Sometimes sharp points of iron were tied on to the ends of the thongs to make its use very, very severe. The SCOURGE was used as a punishment. The person had their arms tied to a low pillar and they had to bend forward with their back left uncovered. Then they were lashed with the SCOURGE. Many times people who were punished this way died. The marks which the SCOURGE made were called STRIPES.

HOW CAN I USE IT?

The Lord Jesus Christ was lashed with a SCOURGE before He was hung on the cross to die for us. In the book of Isaiah chapter 53 verse 5 we read these words - "and with his stripes we are healed". This verse refers to the SCOURGING which Jesus took in order to redeem us. What an awful thing to do to Jesus. Never forget just how much Jesus suffered for you.

SPECIAL ASSIGNMENT OVER PAGE

SPECIAL ASSIGNMENT

SECRET

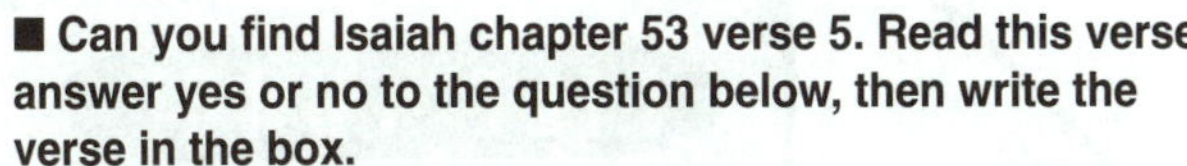

■ **Can you find Isaiah chapter 53 verse 5. Read this verse answer yes or no to the question below, then write the verse in the box.**

Do you love Jesus for doing this for you?

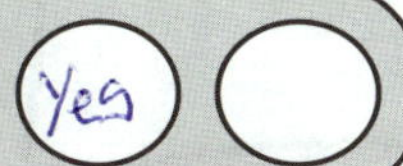

Isaiah 53 V 5:

But he was wounded for my transgressions: he was bruised for our inquities: the Chastisement of our peace was upon him. AND BY HIS STRIPES WE ARE HEALDED

THE S FILES

TOP SECRET

FILE THREE

Spikenard

WHERE CAN I FIND IT?

Isn't this a very strange word! It can be found if you search in the Gospel of John chapter 12 verse 3.

WHAT DOES IT MEAN?

In the verse where you found this word you will have discovered that SPIKENARD was expensive to buy and that it had a strong smell. SPIKENARD is a plant which originally comes from India. It was very precious because it cost so much and it was contained in an airtight box which was sealed. This was to stop it rotting or spilling.

HOW CAN I USE IT?

Not only can you find the word SPIKENARD in the Gospel of John, but you can find it in the Gospel of Mark. Look in chapter 14 verse 3. Here you will learn that the lady who owned this SPIKENARD broke the box it was contained in and used the precious ointment to pour on Jesus' head. This was a very gracious and kind gift which she gave to Jesus.
Our hearts are a bit like a box of precious ointment. We can use what is in them to love and worship God.

ASSIGNMENT [circle your answers]

■ In John 12 vs 1-8 The lady's name was	MARTHA	MARY
● How much spikenard did she use?	A LITRE	A POUND
▲ Which part of Jesus did she pour it over?	HIS FEET	HIS HEAD
■ In Mark 14 vs 3-8 the name of the town was	BETHEL	BETHANY

THE S FILES

CLASSIFIED

FILE FOUR

Scorner

WHERE CAN I FIND IT?

If you search in Proverbs 13 verse 1 you will find the word SCORNER

WHAT DOES IT MEAN?

A SCORNER is a person who laughs at things which are important. A SCORNER also mocks God and the people who love and serve Him. A SCORNER not only pays no heed to God, but they pay no attention to their parents either. SCORNERS are foolish people who won't take good advice from anybody.

HOW CAN I USE IT?

You certainly don't want to be a SCORNER. If you find Psalm 1 verse 1, you can learn that being happy in life depends upon you not being a SCORNER! This verse teaches you that a happy person doesn't keep company with people who are wicked and who mock God.

ASSIGNMENT

- ■ **Read all of Psalm 1 and answer these questions.**
- ● **A happy person loves the W**ord **of God.**
- ◆ **An unhappy person is friendly with S**corners.
- ▲ **A happy person is like a tree planted by the R**iver.
- ● **An unhappy person is like C**haff.
- ■ **Ungody people are wicked and S**inful.

THE T FILES

NEED TO KNOW

FILE ONE

Temptation

WHERE CAN I FIND IT?

This big word TEMPTATION can be found in the book of James. Look in chapter 1 verse 12. Remember James is near the end of the New Testament and it is quite a small book. It has just 5 chapters.

WHAT DOES IT MEAN?

The word TEMPTATION means that we are being PROMPTED or ENCOURAGED to do something UNWISE or WRONG. The person who is enticing us to sin is of course the Devil. For this reason he is called the TEMPTER. He tries to ensnare us or lead us to do wrong.

HOW CAN I USE IT?

It is not a sin to be TEMPTED. It is only a sin if you give in and do the thing which the TEMPTER is wanting you to do. Everybody has been TEMPTED and everybody has been TEMPTED to do the same evil things. But God is more powerful than the Devil and if you listen to Him instead He will help you not to give in to TEMPTATION. In the Lord's Prayer we ask God to keep us from being led into temptation. This is a very important thing to ask God for because He is faithful to us and answers our prayers.

ASSIGNMENT [underline the correct words]

■ **You know the TEMPTER, who is the Devil, even tried to TEMPT the Lord Jesus Christ when He was on earth! Imagine that! Jesus could not sin so it was a pointless task - but the Devil tried anyway. You can read about this for yourself in Matthew chapter four. When you have read about it tick the oval.**

THE T FILES

TOP SECRET

FILE TWO

Tithe

WHERE CAN I FIND IT?

In the very first book of the Bible - Genesis - in chapter 14 verse 20 you will find the word TITHE

WHAT DOES IT MEAN?

A TITHE is a TENTH. When Moses lived he instructed the people to give a tenth of what they had to God. This was a tenth of everything - their cattle, their produce, their land and their money. This was the law and the tenth belonged to the Lord.

HOW CAN I USE IT?

There is no reason why we ought not to give one tenth of our money to God. One tenth isn't very much - it is just 10p out of every pound we have. There are many people who work for God all day every day who need help from us. There are many works which exist which help spread the good news of the Gospel to people. Our money can help those works succeed. God has given us much - isn't it good to be able to give something back to Him?

ASSIGNMENT [circle your answers]

■ A tithe is equal to	A FIFTH	A QUARTER	A TENTH
▲ A tenth of one pound is just	50 PENCE	10 PENCE	20 PENCE

THE T FILES

CLASSIFIED

Tradition

WHERE CAN I FIND IT?

This is quite a big word but it isn't hard to find. Look in Matthew chapter 15 verse 2. In fact it is in verse 3 as well!

WHAT DOES IT MEAN?

A TRADITION is not a law but it is something handed down from generation to generation. It is a CUSTOM. It is something which has been done for many, many years. TRADITIONS are an important part of family life and they have an important role in the country in which you live.

HOW CAN I USE IT?

TRADITIONS are not bad things but they must never be exalted to being something they are not. God's laws or His commandments are the things which we must obey. The authority of the written word of God is the only authority which is given to us. TRADITIONS do not have this authority and never must be given it.

ASSIGNMENT [circle your answers]

■ A TRADITION is a	CHURCH	LAW	CUSTOM
◆ The Bible is my	TRADITION	CULTURE	AUTHORITY
▲ I obey God's	TRADITION	WORD	CULTURE
▼ I do not obey man's	CULTURE	TRADITIONS	CHURCH

THE T FILES

NEED TO KNOW

FILE FOUR

Transfigured

WHERE CAN I FIND IT?

This is a massive word! And it has an amazing meaning. Let's find it first. Look in Matthew chapter 17 verse 2. You won't miss it, it's so big!

WHAT DOES IT MEAN?

When something is transfigured, its APPEARANCE is changed. The Lord Jesus Christ was TRANSFIGURED. He became extremely majestic and glorious. His face shone like the sun and his robes glistened. And God said that Jesus was His "beloved son in whom he was well pleased". Peter, James and John, three of Jesus' disciples all saw this happen to Jesus.

HOW CAN I USE IT?

As children of God, we can by faith see this beauty of Jesus. He is sinless, and He loves us everlastingly! He died for us and He prays for us. His spirit dwells in us to be with us on earth until He comes back again. The countenance, or the face of Jesus, should always shine in beauty for us.

ASSIGNMENT [fill in the gaps]

■ When Jesus was T _ _ _ _ _ _ _ _ _ _ _ _ _ _
His appearance was changed.

THE U FILES

SECRET

FILE ONE

Undergirding

WHERE CAN I FIND IT?

If you look in Acts chapter 27 verse 17 you will find this big word UNDERGIRDING.

WHAT DOES IT MEAN?

UNDERGIRDING is when a ship is encircled with cable to strengthen it. Perhaps the ship has been weakened in a storm or faces a storm, the undergirding is to help it and secure it as best as possible.

HOW CAN I USE IT?

The promises of God are like UNDERGIRDING. They strengthen us when we have been disappointed and they help us when we are in the middle of a rough patch! Because of this it is important to KNOW God's promises. For example, God has said that He will never leave us nor forsake us. Do you know that promise?

ASSIGNMENT [tick box]

■ **Find this wonderful promise. Search for it in Hebrews chapter 13 verse 5. When you find it, read it carefully and tick this circle. Remember it is God's special promise to you!**

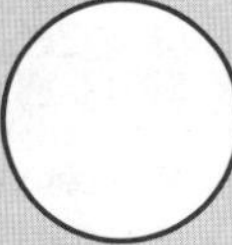

THE U FILES

CLASSIFIED

FILE TWO

Usury

WHERE CAN I FIND IT?

If you look in Matthew chapter 25 verse 27 you will find this word USURY.

WHAT DOES IT MEAN?

In the Hebrew language the word USURY means BITING! In the Bible, a person who loaned money to someone and charged them high interest was severely denounced. What they were doing was lending money to the poor and then making them pay back far, far more than was loaned. They were taking advantage of those in need and just like the Hebrew word says, they were BITING or hurting them.

HOW CAN I USE IT?

Today the word USURY really means UNLAWFULLY making money, or making exorbitant claims on people to whom money has been loaned. Exorbitant means outrageous. This is a wrong practice and it displeases God. The money which we have we are responsible for, and we must not use it to hurt others. There is nothing at all wrong with having money and there is nothing at all wrong with having lots of money. But it is wrong to think that money is more important than anything else.

ASSIGNMENT [tick box]

■ **The word money can be found in I Timothy chapter 6 verse 10. This verse tells us that the love of money is the root of all evil. When you read it why don't you tick the box beside this bag of money.**

THE U FILES

TOP SECRET

Undertake

WHERE CAN I FIND IT?

In the book of Isaiah chapter 38 verse 14 you will see this word UNDERTAKE. It comes almost at the end of the verse.

WHAT DOES IT MEAN?

To UNDERTAKE means to TAKE RESPONSIBILITY for someone or something. You might UNDERTAKE to do a job. This means that you ENTER UPON A PROMISE to do the work.

HOW CAN I USE IT?

Jesus Christ UNDERTOOK the responsibility of our sins when He died on the cross. He became our SURETY. That means He was responsible for the debt of our sins! That was the biggest UNDERTAKING of all. He was responsible for the price of the sins of the whole world!

ASSIGNMENT

John 3 verse 16 teaches us exactly what was UNDERTAKEN by Jesus, and it also teaches us how we can know that our sins have been paid for. This is an excellent verse to learn. When you have it learned, close your Bible and write it down in the big box on the next page.
Will you UNDERTAKE to do this?

SECRET

TOP SECRET

FILE FOUR

Upbraid

WHERE CAN I FIND IT?

You have found lots of words now in the book of Matthew, so this one should be nice and easy for you! Look for the word UPBRAID in chapter 11 verse 20.

WHAT DOES IT MEAN?

UPBRAID means to SCOLD or to REPROACH. Reproach is another word for REBUKE. I'm sure you have been UPBRAIDED once or twice! I don't really like being scolded, do you?!

HOW CAN I USE IT?

In the book of James, chapter 1 verse 5 we learn about something which God will never scold us for doing. Can you guess what it might be?

ASSIGNMENT [fill in the gaps]

■ **Find James chapter 1 verse 5. When you read it fill in the gaps**

■ **If I ask God for** W _ _ _ _ _

◆ **He will give it to me** L _ _ _ _ _ _ _ _ _

▲ **And will not** U _ _ _ _ _ _ _ ME

THE V FILES

NEED TO KNOW

FILE ONE

Viol

WHERE CAN I FIND IT?

This little word can be found in the book of Amos. Amos is in the Old Testament in between Joel and Obadiah. Look for the word VIOL in chapter 6 verse 5.

WHAT DOES IT MEAN?

A VIOL is a stringed instrument or a lyre. It is not unlike a harp.

HOW CAN I USE IT?

The lyre, the harp and the VIOL are all used in worship. Music is a beautiful gift. Some people are very talented at music. Others may not be good at actually playing music, but they appreciate it nonetheless. Wouldn't the world be a dull place without music? Even the birds wouldn't sing! It is important that we have a good standard of music when we worship God. Not just any old tune misplayed will do! God delights when we order our worship correctly and it gives Him pleasure that those who have talents in music are encouraged to use them for Him.

ASSIGNMENT [memory test]

■ **Here is a lovely verse from a hymn. It has the word viol in it. Maybe you could find out the tune too!**

"With harps and with viols
There stands a great throng
In the presence of Jesus
And this is their song -
Unto Him who hath loved us
And washed us from sin
Unto Him be the glory
Forever Amen."

THE V FILES

TOP SECRET

FILE TWO

Virtue

WHERE CAN I FIND IT?

This word VIRTUE can mean two different things so you will need to find it in two places to understand this. First of all look for it in Mark chapter 5 verse 30. Then look for it in second Peter chapter 1 verse 3.

WHAT DOES IT MEAN?

VIRTUE may mean POWER or it may mean GOODNESS. In the first verse where you found this word (Mark 5:30) it means POWER. In the second verse it means GOODNESS. It is really by this second meaning which we know the word VIRTUE today.

HOW CAN I USE IT?

God wants from us a very simple thing. He wants us to be GOOD. Now you can't get more straightforward than that, can you? But then the devil sticks his oar in and he makes it hard for us to be good and to do good. And big stupid you and me - what do we do, we listen to the devil and make things hard for ourselves! And all God wants is for us to be good. It's really not too much to ask, now is it?

ASSIGNMENT [fill in the gaps]

■ Virtue = G _ _ _ _ _ _ _

❖ God is pleased when I am G _ _ _

▲ God is G _ _ _

▼ I want to obey G _ _ _

THE V FILES

SECRET

FILE THREE

Vengeance

WHERE CAN I FIND IT?

Look in Romans chapter 12 verse 19 for this big word VENGEANCE.

WHAT DOES IT MEAN?

VENGEANCE means PUNISHMENT. VENGEANCE is the exclusive right of God. He will vindicate the person who is right and He will punish the person who has done wrong. Vindicate means to clear of charges or to establish who is honest.

HOW CAN I USE IT?

Throughout our lives we will meet people who do wrong to us. It might be a small wrong or it might be a big wrong. Often we will be upset and even very angry about this. But we are taught that we are not to seek revenge. That is, we are not to go about arranging their punishment. God will see to that. He will show you to be right and the wrongdoer to be wrong. What is more, He will proceed with a course of action which will punish them. Now do you see how important it is not to do wrong to others? If you do, God is obliged to punish you. But do you also see how good it is to do right? You never have to worry about revenge on others. God sorts all that out.

ASSIGNMENT [underline your answer]

■ VENGEANCE means	PATIENCE	PUNISHMENT	VIRTUE
▲ VENGEANCE belongs to	MAN	WOMAN	GOD

THE V FILES

CLASSIFIED

FILE FOUR

Vagabond

WHERE CAN I FIND IT?

You can find the word VAGABOND in the very first book of the Bible, Genesis. Look for it in chapter 4 verse 12. If you like you can find it again in verse 14 as well.

WHAT DOES IT MEAN?

A VAGABOND is a WANDERER or a FUGITIVE. This means they have no permanent home. They roam from place to place and are an outsider wherever they go.

HOW CAN I USE IT?

When Cain murdered his brother Abel, God cursed him and told him that he would be a VAGABOND, an OUTSIDER. Before we ask Jesus to redeem us we are OUTSIDERS. We are WANDERING and lost and alone. When He redeems us - all of this changes. He takes us into His family, He gives us a home in Heaven for eternity and we are no longer lost and alone. There are many poor, lonely, vagabonds in this world. They desperately need to hear about Jesus. Your friends and neighbours need to hear about Jesus. We need to keep our eyes open for VAGABONDS, for people who are lost in their sins. We need to pray for them. We need to befriend them. And we need to tell them about Jesus.

ASSIGNMENT [circle your answer]

■ **Pick out four things which you can do for VAGABONDS**

PRAY FOR THEM **IGNORE THEM** **BEFRIEND THEM**

HELP THEM **TELL THEM ABOUT JESUS** **FORGET THEM**

NB. Vagabonds are often well disguised. There might even be one in your Church!

THE W FILES

NEED TO KNOW

FILE ONE

Withs

WHERE CAN I FIND IT?

Now here's a funny wee word - WITHS. If you look in Judges chapter 16 verse 7 you will find it.

WHAT DOES IT MEAN?

WITHS are pliable TWIGS which are twisted closely together while green and used the way rope would be used. They are made into small cords which can tie or bind things.

HOW CAN I USE IT?

In the chapter in Judges where you found this wee word WITHS, you will realise that this word is in the story of Samson. Imagine a great big strong man like Samson being tied up with little cords made from twigs! Samson broke those cords as though they were threads! But of course the story of Samson has very sad parts in it. The mighty Samson was weakened and captured by his enemies. Just like Samson, we can easily be weakened by giving in to temptation and doing wrong. Sometimes just a tiny wee thing trips us up!

ASSIGNMENT [circle your answer]

■ **We must always be watchful for Satan would try to tie us in knots just as the Philistines tried to tie Samson with WITHS.**
▲ **Why don't you read the story of Samson and give yourself a big smile in this space when you do.**

THE W FILES

SECRET

FILE TWO

Witnesses

WHERE CAN I FIND IT?

If you search in Isaiah chapter 44 verse 8 you will find the word WITNESSES.

WHAT DOES IT MEAN?

A WITNESS is a person who gives TESTIMONY or confirms the EVIDENCE which is presented to them. They give a TRUTHFUL ACCOUNT of something that has happened.

HOW CAN I USE IT?

We are God's WITNESSES! You read that fact in the verse you found in Isaiah. When we are redeemed we are able to give a truthful account to others of what the Lord Jesus Christ has done for us. A WITNESS who keeps quiet is of no use at all!

ASSIGNMENT [circle your answer]

■ Here is another fact to learn about the word WITNESS. In the book of Romans chapter 8 verse 16 we are told that the Holy Spirit is a WITNESS to the fact that we are children of God!
Maybe you could find this verse and learn it. When you have it learned - give yourself a big star here.

THE W FILES

TOP SECRET

FILE THREE

Wimples

WHERE CAN I FIND IT?

You should be able to find Isaiah really easily now as you have searched out lots of words in it. This word WIMPLES can be found in chapter three verse 22.

WHAT DOES IT MEAN?

A WIMPLE is a HOOD or a HEADDRESS. It is like a shawl which comes up over the head. Today, the hoods which nuns wear are called WIMPLES.

HOW CAN I USE IT?

A WIMPLE is a covering. It is a covering just like a hat, or a cap. It doesn't do anything other than keep the person's head warm. That is all it does. We have a very special covering don't we? It is the covering of the blood of Jesus. This covering cleanses our sins and makes us pure. This covering is called IMPUTED RIGHTEOUSNESS. It is given to us by Christ. It is much better than a WIMPLE!

ASSIGNMENT [fill in the gaps]

- **When I become a child of God I am made**

R _ _ _ _ _ _ _ _ _ _ _ _ _ _ . This is called I _ _ _ _ _ _

Righteousness because it is given to me by Christ.

THE W FILES

NEED TO KNOW

FILE FOUR

Wormwood

WHERE CAN I FIND IT?

If you look in Proverbs chapter 5 verse 4 you will find the word WORMWOOD.

WHAT DOES IT MEAN?

WORMWOOD is a plant which is known for its EXTREME BITTERNESS. It also is a very dangerous plant as some species of it can kill.

HOW CAN I USE IT?

The bitterness of WORMWOOD is like the wicked. Those who disobey God, not only hurt themselves but they also hurt others. In contrast to this, those who listen to and obey God are not a bit like WORMWOOD. Remember the lovely tree which you read about in Psalm 1? That is what those who love God are like - a beautiful green tree, not a disgusting, bitter old plant.

ASSIGNMENT [location test]

■ **How about reading Psalm 1 again just to remind you how much of a difference there is between the Godly and the un-godly.**
When you have read it, why don't you fill in the little certificate on the next page

CLASSIFIED

This is to certify that I

____

have read Psalm One and know the difference between the godly and the ungodly.

BLUE RIBBON PERFORMANCE !

NEED TO KNOW

There are **none** -

that was **easy** wasn't it!

SPECIAL NOTE

You are almost at the end of the alphabet and your word search is almost over.

You have just **two** short files left - Y and Z

Both are very brief.

Are you **ready?**

Prepare to **complete** your

word search mission!

THE Y FILES

SECRET

FILE ONE

Yoke

WHERE CAN I FIND IT?

Turn to Matthew chapter 11 and verses 29-30. If you read these you will discover the word YOKE.

WHAT DOES IT MEAN?

A YOKE was a DEVICE which was laid upon the neck of a beast such as an ox or a horse. It was fastened both to the animal and to the plough. This meant when the animal walked it pulled the plough along for the farmer.

HOW CAN I USE IT?

Jesus explains to us, using the idea of a YOKE, that we are servants of His. Just as the horse or ox served the farmer, so too we serve Jesus. But there is a difference - the YOKE animals had to wear was heavy and the plough which they had to pull was heavy. The YOKE of service which we take is not like this at all. The verse teaches us that it is an EASY YOKE and a LIGHT BURDEN. That is because it is not ours - it is His - He says, 'My yoke is easy and my burden is light.'

ASSIGNMENT

■ **Do you work for Jesus everyday? You can do this by being kind to others, helpful to your family, obedient to your parents, loving to God's creatures. Why don't you think of THREE other ways you can work for Jesus. When you do tick this box.** ☐

THE Z FILES

TOP SECRET

FILE ONE

Zealously

WHERE CAN I FIND IT?

In the New Testament book of Galatians chapter four verse 18 you will find the word ZEALOUSLY.

WHAT DOES IT MEAN?

ZEALOUS means ENTHUSIASTIC. So ZEALOUSLY means that someone is doing something with great keenness or enthusiasm. They cannot hide their earnestness. They are full of ZEAL, full of fervour!

HOW CAN I USE IT?

The verse where you found the word ZEALOUSLY tells us that it is good to be enthusiastic about good itself!
Many people will tell you that good is dull and boring. That's a load of nonsense. Good is exciting, and good is a challenge, and good is something to be ZEALOUS or enthusiastic about!

ASSIGNMENT [learning test]

■ **Why don't you make this verse in Galatians your motto? Let's be enthusiastic about good! Copy the verse into the motto tag on the next page.**

TOP SECRET

My special disciple's MOTTO is

Galatians 4 verse 18

NEXT

Well done little disciple! You have completed the POWER WORD FILES. Now we come to the CONCEPTS.

Are you prepared? Let's get searching and learning

Extra Info Concept FILES

ANGELS

An angel is a messenger, but it is a very unusual messenger because it is a spiritual being. Angels are God's special agents. They are a race of creatures which God has exalted or placed above human beings in the scale of existence. Just as we are above the animal kingdom, angels are above the human race. The angels in Heaven have never sinned but they are not to be worshipped by us the way we worship God. Angels serve God and carry out His instructions. In the Bible angels appeared in shining raiment and brought messages from God to people on earth. It was an angel who told Mary that she was going to give birth to Jesus. As God's children we are privileged to have angels guarding and protecting us. So always remember that angels are obedient, sinless servants of God and that they are real and very beautiful creatures. When we die, angels will carry us to Heaven. When we are in Heaven angels will be our companions.

CLASSIFIED

ATONEMENT

Somebody made amends for our wrong doing. Somebody put right what our sins made wrong. That somebody was Jesus Christ. And, what He did is called ATONEMENT. Jesus ATONED for our sins. He ATONED for them by shedding His precious blood and dying on the cross. So our ATONEMENT was a very costly business. It caused Jesus to suffer great agony. It cost Him His life.

The word ATONEMENT is made up like this. AT ONE MENT. When two people are reconciled they are made to be at-one. They are in agreement with one another. Our ATONEMENT does exactly this. It unites us or makes us at-one with God. Our sins are covered by the blood of Jesus and we are covered by His righteousness. There is no other way to be atoned than this. The death of Jesus Christ is offered to God for our ATONEMENT, and REDEMPTION is given to us as a result of it.

C

COMMUNION

Do you know that there is a difference between talking to someone and communing with someone?

If we COMMUNE with someone we are talking to them in an intense or in an intimate way. We forget about everything else that is going on and our whole mind is occupied or taken up with that person. The result of this is that we are very close friends with the person we are able to COMMUNE with. Very often you will hear people use the word FELLOWSHIP. Usually this means a unique or special friendship as a result of COMMUNION with God. You don't have to be a grown-up to commune with God. You don't have to be a man or a minister to COMMUNE with God. A child, a man, a woman, any one in fact can COMMUNE with God. He can be our special friend if we talk to Him about all the things which matter to us.

There is also a very special way in which the word COMMUNION is used. It refers to what is called an ORDINANCE. An ordinance is something which God has appointed or instructed us to do. THE ORDINANCE OF THE LORD'S SUPPER or COMMUNION is the way in which we remember the death of Jesus Christ, the only Son of God. To do this we eat bread and drink wine. The bread makes us remember how the body of Jesus was hurt and injured when He died for us.

C

COMMUNION CONTINUED

The wine represents the blood of Jesus which He shed for us to cleanse away our sins. In COMMUNION these things - bread and wine - are what we call symbols. They are not the body and the blood of Jesus, they are simply two earthly things which serve to remind us of what Jesus did for us.

Now there is one other thing which you should know about these two aspects of communion. In order to do both of these things - that is -

1. To commune WITH God

2. To TAKE communion

you need to be a "CHILD OF GOD".
Remember what you learned about the word ANATHEMA? You cannot be forgotten by God if you love Him. If you love Him you are a child of God and that, you see, is the key to communion.

C

COVENANT

A covenant is really a promise or a bond. Often a covenant is accompanied by something which serves as a reminder of the promise. For example, the rainbow is a reminder of God's promise never to destroy the earth by a flood. God covenanted with Noah that He would not do to the earth again what had been done in the flood. Another example of something which serves to remind us of a promise made is a wedding ring. When two people marry they promise to love one another and the rings which they wear are a sign or a reminder of that promise.

The covenant which has the greatest impact upon our lives is the covenant which was made to us on the cross by Jesus Christ. This covenant promises us salvation and eternal life and it was sealed or confirmed by the blood of Jesus.

This covenant is sometimes referred to as the NEW COVENANT and it depends completely upon the work of Christ, not upon any good deeds or works which we may do. This is why Christians are sometimes called covenanters or children of the covenant.

CLASSIFIED

DEVOTION

If you are devoted to someone or some thing it means you are very enthusiastic about that person or thing. You love it or them very much indeed. Your devotion makes you loyal. There is nothing wrong with devotion to a person or a cause. Nothing at all. In fact, it is a very good thing and it can bring much enjoyment. But it would be completely ruined if your devotion to that person or thing was more important than your devotion to God who gave it to you in the first place! Remember the first commandment which you found in Exodus 20? This very first rule says - no other gods before Me. So, any thing or any person, no matter how decent and good they are, must not become of greater importance to us than God.

Now, there is a way to ensure this. To keep God first means that you must be devoted to Him first. To do this is very simple - you get to know Him. You listen to Him and you talk to Him, just as you listen and talk to people you love. You listen to His words. God's words are written in the Bible for us - so that makes it very straightforward. You talk to Him in prayer - and that isn't hard either. So devotion to God isn't a difficult thing to fit into your life at all. Besides, as you get to know Him you will look forward to this time with Him every day. Always remember, God is with you all day every day so you be sure and take advantage of His company!

FORGIVENESS

The forgiveness of our sins is the exclusive or special right of God. Nobody or nothing else can forgive our sins. Our forgiveness is full, free and everlasting and it is the result of what Jesus Christ did on the cross for us.

When we are forgiven the great debt of our sins, we are able to have in our lives a forgiving spirit or attitude to others who do wrong to us. This does not mean that we have to like the wrong-doer. It does not mean that we have to say they are nice when clearly they are not at all nice! But it does mean that we can dislike the wicked, hurtful and cruel things that they do, without wishing harm on them in eternity. They may have to be punished for their wrong-doing but we should not wish them separated from God for eternity. It is not an easy thing to forgive but it is not an impossible thing either. And, like many things we must learn to do, we must learn to be forgiving. If we don't forgive others, we won't be forgiven ourselves. That is pretty straightforward isn't it? The Lord's prayer teaches us this fact - “forgive us our trespasses as we forgive others”.

Of course, it is much easier to learn something hard by starting with something small. So when it comes to forgiveness start by forgiving the little things that need forgiving and you will find when the big things come along you are much better prepared.

HEAVEN

HEAVEN is the place which we will inhabit after we die, along with all others who are redeemed. In this place there are many mansions prepared for Christ's friends and followers. No effects of sin will be found in HEAVEN. Jesus is there and we will serve God in HEAVEN. This gift of eternal life in HEAVEN has been made possible by Jesus Christ's death for us. I really look forward to HEAVEN, do you? HEAVEN is going to be fantastic. It will be even more beautiful than this world. There will be colours which we cannot possibly imagine and there will be precious stones that the City is built with that we have never seen before. There will be no tarmac on the streets of HEAVEN - but real gold! It really will be an amazing place to live and we will live there for ever and ever and ever. Of course the best thing about HEAVEN is that Jesus will be there. There will be no sickness, no sadness and no sin there. We will enjoy happiness forever and never be tired. Every day of your life here on earth you should think about the place of your future life. Your life on earth is preparing you or making you ready for your future in HEAVEN. If you remind yourself of this each day it will certainly help you to be a very happy Christian while still on earth.

TOP SECRET

CLASSIFIED

HELL

When we talk about the future we mean the time after the present. At present we live on this wonderful planet called earth which God created for us. But, in the future after we die we will live our eternal life in Heaven or in Hell. HELL is the future place where the ungodly will exist. This place called HELL is a place of separation. It is a place which keeps the ungodly separated from God forever and ever. This place called HELL is a place of suffering and remorse. Those who go there will regret for all eternity that they did not accept the offer of salvation which Christ made to them. When we learn about Hell in the Bible it is described to us very vividly. It is made extremely clear to us what happens if we reject Jesus Christ. So, you see, we know fine well the end result of being evil. It isn't hidden from us. It isn't a surprise sprung upon us. Our future can be in Heaven with Christ or in HELL separated from Him. It might not be very nice to think about such an awful place but it would be far, far worse to not consider it and spend your future there! If you want to spend your future there you are absolutely mad. I want none of that thank you, not when Heaven is the other choice, and what's more, I don't want my family, my friends or my neighbours to have their future in Hell either. So I need to pray for them and ask Jesus to redeem them if they aren't already His children. And I also must be very sure that I am a good example as a child of God, otherwise it would totally put them off the idea of following Him too.

JUSTIFICATION

If you or I were a castaway we would be what is described as CONDEMNED. We would not be APPROVED by God. But God doesn't want to reject us! After all, He loved us so much that He sent Jesus to die for us. He did this to take away our CONDEMNATION or to pardon us from our sins. Jesus paid the debt of our sins. Then He offered to us that payment as a RANSOM. This ransom FREED us from having to pay for our own sins.

The word JUSTIFICATION is the OPPOSITE of the word CONDEMNED. You see, when God forgives or pardons us for our sins, He treats us AS IF WE HAD NEVER SINNED. This is called JUSTIFICATION. And, because there is no way of being pardoned except by believing in the Lord Jesus Christ, it is called JUSTIFICATION BY FAITH. Faith is trust. We trust or believe that God forgives our sins when we ask Him.

A very easy way to remember the meaning of this big word JUSTIFICATION is to learn this - when I am JUSTIFIED it's "just as if I'd never sinned."

SECRET

CLASSIFIED

LAW

In the Bible the word law has several uses. You have found many words in the book of Psalms. When you read about the law of God in the Psalms it usually means all the things which God put in place to keep the world in order and which we need to obey.

The Law of God also refers to the ten commandments which are rules or laws that we live by.

But the laws of God do not redeem us. Simply obeying God's laws will not forgive us our sins! Doing good things will not cleanse us from our wrong-doing. We depend upon Jesus Christ for all that. And, while the laws of God don't take us to Heaven, they do become our duty to obey. We conform to God's laws when we become a child of God. This does not make our lives dull and boring and hard. In fact it does just the opposite, it makes them very pleasant. You see, God's laws prevent us making a mess of things and there's nothing worse than a mess of a life!

MORALS

MORALS are based on the difference between good and evil. They are the STANDARDS by which we live.

A moral person for example, is an honest person and their character is pure. A person who is not moral bases their life on standards which are not right. The standards which God gives us are the ten commandments. It is from these we learn good MORAL behaviour. As you grow older the importance of MORALITY becomes greater because you take on new responsibilities. You will get a job and in your work it is necessary to be MORAL and honest. You will make many friends and you ought to act in a MORAL or a right way towards the people with whom you are friendly. You will perhaps meet someone who becomes a special friend that you love very much. You need to have good standards or MORALS in order to keep your love for that person special.

So MORALS are the principles or standards by which we live. Good behaviour not only makes us kind to others, it keeps our own lives tidy and a tidy life is much easier to look after than a dishonest untidy life that always needs sorted out!

TOP SECRET

PRAYER

PRAYER is the word which is used to explain how we TALK TO, or COMMUNE WITH, God. It is a very precious gift and we are free to use it as often as we wish, every hour of our lives!

Usually when we think about prayer we think about ASKING. Prayer may be used by us to ASK our Heavenly Father for things. This is an important aspect or part of prayer and it is a good and proper thing to ASK God. But, there are other things which are important also. It is important to THANK God for things too, for things which are so common we almost forget about them. These usually are the most valuable things which He gives us every day. So it is good to ASK God for things and it is good to THANK God for things. Even better though, it is good to just SEEK GOD'S COMPANY. By prayer we can simply enjoy TELLING GOD WE ADORE HIM. We can let Him know that we love Him very deeply. If you use your prayers first of all to WORSHIP Him then you will learn that when you do ASK for things, you will ask for the things which God Himself wants to give you. How do I know this? I learn this when I read John chapter 15 verse seven. John is one of the four books which come right at the beginning of the New Testament. These four books - Matthew, Mark, Luke and John are often called the Gospels. This particular verse in John (chapter 15:7) teaches us that by abiding, or living, in Jesus we are able to ask God for the things He can give us. The very first step you must take to abide in Him is to become one of His children.

PRAYER CONTINUED

There is another verse which you might like to find as well. This verse is in the book of Romans (Romans comes just two books after John). Find chapter 8, and read verse 26. This verse explains that the Holy Spirit helps us to know WHAT WE SHOULD PRAY FOR, and what is more, it tells us that the Holy Spirit itself makes intercession for us. All that may seem a bit difficult to understand! So, put simply, it means that Jesus Christ Himself talks to God on our behalf! He explains to God much better than we ever could, what we really are asking for. That's a great relief, isn't it?! Jesus, Who loved us so much that He died for us, now continues to help us by praying for us. All the things that we find hard to explain to God when we pray, Jesus sorts out for us by praying far better than we ever could!
So you see, when you talk to God you are being like His Son Jesus. And there is no better person to be like!

PROPITIATION

What a mouthful this word is! But, when you learn what it means you will agree that it tastes very good!

In the New Testament there are three books called John. The fourth New Testament book is called John or the Gospel of John. But if you go on over, past the books called first and second Peter, where you found the word ADVERSARY, you will come to three more books called John - first John, second and third John. Now search for chapter two of first John and read verse two. Do you see this grand word "Propitiation"?

Now, you already know that Christ is your ADVOCATE, your DEFENDER. Well, this word explains how He became your ADVOCATE.

PROPITIATION is the action of a person who, by doing a specific thing, makes peace with another person who has cause to be offended. Let's use some names to explain this action.

JESUS CHRIST DIED on the cross to take the punishment for our sins AND MADE PEACE WITH GOD Who was offended or hurt by our sins.

This action made Jesus Christ the PROPITIATION for our sins. The One Who stood in for us, and Who stood in for the sins of the whole world!

RESURRECTION

Jesus Christ rose from the dead! It is through the death and resurrection of Christ that our salvation is secured. If Jesus had died for us but was unable to come alive again, then death would have been more powerful than Him. But Jesus Christ won the victory over death, and His resurrection assures us that we too will be resurrected to spend eternity with Him! Jesus was resurrected three days after His death, and forty days after His resurrection He ascended into Heaven. That is where Jesus is now, preparing Heaven for us and interceding or talking to God His Father about us and our needs. Then the wonderful thing is that He is coming back to earth again at the end of the world. Just like Jesus, we also will be resurrected and our bodies will no longer have disease or pain. We will have new spiritual bodies which will be ours for all eternity and we will serve God and enjoy heaven all because Jesus rose from the dead! Isn't the resurrection a wonderful thing?

CONFIDENTIAL

RIGHTEOUSNESS

In the Bible you will learn about qualities which belong to God. These characteristics of God are what we call the ATTRIBUTES of God. They are the things which make up His character.

RIGHTEOUSNESS is an ATTRIBUTE of God. It is part of His being. It is His nature.

RIGHTEOUSNESS is a big word which includes things like holiness, goodness, justice, and faithfulness. It tells us about the greatness of God. This is what makes God the King of kings.

Sometimes in life you may hear a person being described as a RIGHTEOUS man or woman. This is our way of saying that the person is upright, that they are fair-minded and deal honestly with others. It is something we should seek to be.

However, God's RIGHTEOUSNESS is given to us in a special way. When we ask Him to forgive us our sins and accept Him as Lord then He IMPUTES HIS RIGHTEOUSNESS to us. This means He clothes us with a RIGHTEOUSNESS which is not our own. It is His gift to us. He replaces the guilt of our sin with the covering of His goodness! This righteousness is called IMPUTED RIGHTEOUSNESS and it means He PUTS His goodness onto us.

TABERNACLE

This word means a tent or a moveable dwelling place. The first tabernacle was a very ornate tent made to particular instructions. These instructions were given to Moses in Mount Sinai. You can read all about these details in EXODUS CHAPTER 25 VERSES 9-40. Nowadays our churches are a bit like the tabernacle. They are the buildings where we go to worship God and to meet with other people who also worship Him. Church is also a place where we learn about God's Son, Jesus Christ.

There is also a way in which we ourselves are like a tabernacle! You see, the Holy Spirit, Who was left on earth with us after Jesus returned to Heaven, needs somewhere to live. God has provided a special place for Him in our hearts. If we ask Him, He will dwell in us and be our friend. This spirit is a very gentle being and it is His friendship which helps us to do right. We should be very careful to have the Holy Spirit as our friend.

So, a tabernacle is a place that God lives or dwells. It can be a building or it can even be you and me!

CLASSIFIED

CLASSIFIED

TALENTS

Have you ever been told that you are a very talented person? Or, perhaps you have heard that said about someone else. It really means that the person is GIFTED. Maybe they can play football exceptionally well. Maybe it's the violin or the piano that they can play well. Whatever it is they do, they are said to have A TALENT OR A GIFT for it.

Long ago TALENTS were WEIGHTS and used like money. Talents WEIGHED AROUND 50 TO 100 POUNDS. Gold talents therefore were very valuable. Some talents were silver and although not as valuable as gold talents, they were still worth having!

In the book of Matthew, which you know is the very first book of the New Testament, there is a story all about talents. Why don't you find this chapter and see how many times the word talent is used in it. When you read this parable or story which Jesus told, you will learn that God has given us all talents and it is important that we use very well these things which we are very good at.

Why don't you think about what talents you have and see how you can use them, improve them, and help others with them. You will find an amazing thing when you do this! Your talents will grow! One talent well used will teach you about another one and so on. Goodness, by the time you are ninety you will have talents coming out of your ears!!

CONFIDENTIAL

TRUTH

Truth is exact. It is accurate. Anything which is not true is unclear and confusing. Now, of course you can have a very clear lie told to you but it will contaminate or make dirty the truth and no matter how clearly the lie has been stated, it will make everything else confused. No lie is of the truth. Lies are a bit like chewing gum. You can't swallow chewing gum. If you take it out of your mouth it sticks to your fingers. If you get it off your fingers and stick it somewhere else it creates an awful mess. If you stick it on to a radiator it goes soft and gooey and when something else comes in contact with it, it gets all the gunge over it too. If you were to stick it in your hair - what a disaster! If you were to put it behind your ear - goodness knows how you'd ever get rid of it! If you step onto it your shoe has to be cleaned. You know, it costs thousands of pounds to have chewing gum cleaned off the streets every year! Lies are just like that and if you ever get one in your mouth you had better not let it out! The only safe way to get rid of gum is to spit it into a wrapper and put it into the bin. The wrapper stops it sticking to anything else.

Well, lies need to be all wrapped up in the truth because the truth is the only thing that stops lies sticking. No matter how tempted you are to tell a lie, even a wee one, remember it will stick to another one and another one and another one. Before you know it, the truth is lost and everyone is confused and hurt and entangled. Truth is not messy and truth is clean. Truth keeps you free!

UNPARDONABLE SIN

Blasphemy is when we say untrue, unkind and evil things about God. When we are not children of God and do this, the kindness of God allows Him to forgive us when we repent or say sorry for doing so. When we become children of God, because we love Him and know how good He is, we no longer are careless about His name.
Now it is important to understand that when we talk about God that we remember God is one part of the TRINITY. Trinity means THREE - God is one of three. The Trinity is:-

GOD THE FATHER
GOD THE SON
and GOD THE HOLY GHOST (or the Holy Spirit)

There is a unique and awful sin which is called the UNPARDONABLE SIN. That means it is a sin which God cannot pardon or forgive. He cannot overlook it. This sin is a sin of free or open speech against God the Holy Ghost. It means that a person who SAYS the actions of the Holy Ghost are the actions of the Devil, cannot be forgiven. You see if someone links the Holy Spirit with the power of Satan they are accusing God of being in league with the Devil. God and the Devil can never work together. God is all goodness and the Devil is all wickedness.

UNPARDONABLE SIN CONTINUED

There are two important things to learn about the UNPARDONABLE SIN

No.1 It is a sin of speech
No. 2 To commit this sin the person must wilfully decide to be opposed to God.

These are hard things to understand but it is important for you to know about this sin because Satan is very clever! He would like to make you think that you are guilty of the unpardonable sin! He would like you to think that God can never forgive you. This would upset and worry you - and that's just what he wants - the bad old rip!

But, remember you know that God is good and that He loves you with an EVERLASTING LOVE! What is more, He died to forgive you all your sins and when you love Him you are kept safe from saying wicked things about God the Father, God the Son and God the Holy Ghost.

NEED TO KNOW

VICTORY

Victory is something which you can practice every day. It means success. Success results from making the right choices. For example, if you want to be successful at football you have to spend time playing it and learning to be skilful. You will never be good at it if you don't choose to work at it. If you want to pass your exams at school you have to choose to spend time listening to your teachers and doing your homework. This same principle applies to your life. If you want a successful life, you have to choose to do right. Now, doing right won't always mean you are popular! It won't always mean everyone else will agree with you! But it will mean that you will have victory or success over sin. You will be the winner when it comes to temptation!
When Jesus died for us He had a major battle on His hands. Death wanted to keep Him. Satan wanted death to keep Him captured forever. That way Satan could control the world. But Jesus was more powerful than death and He rose victorious from death and ascended into heaven to be with God the Father.

This victory that Jesus won means that every day we can be successful in saying no to the devil and yes to God because Jesus is alive! Do you want to be a victor? A victor is a champion. A victor is successful. A victor is a winner.

That sounds alright to me!

SPECIAL TASK

There are many more words in the Bible which you may wish to search for now by yourself. We have only looked at some and learned their meaning. Why don't you make up your own power-words file. You don't have to do all the letters at once! As you discover or hear new words write them into these pages along with their meaning.

My own FILES

A

B

C

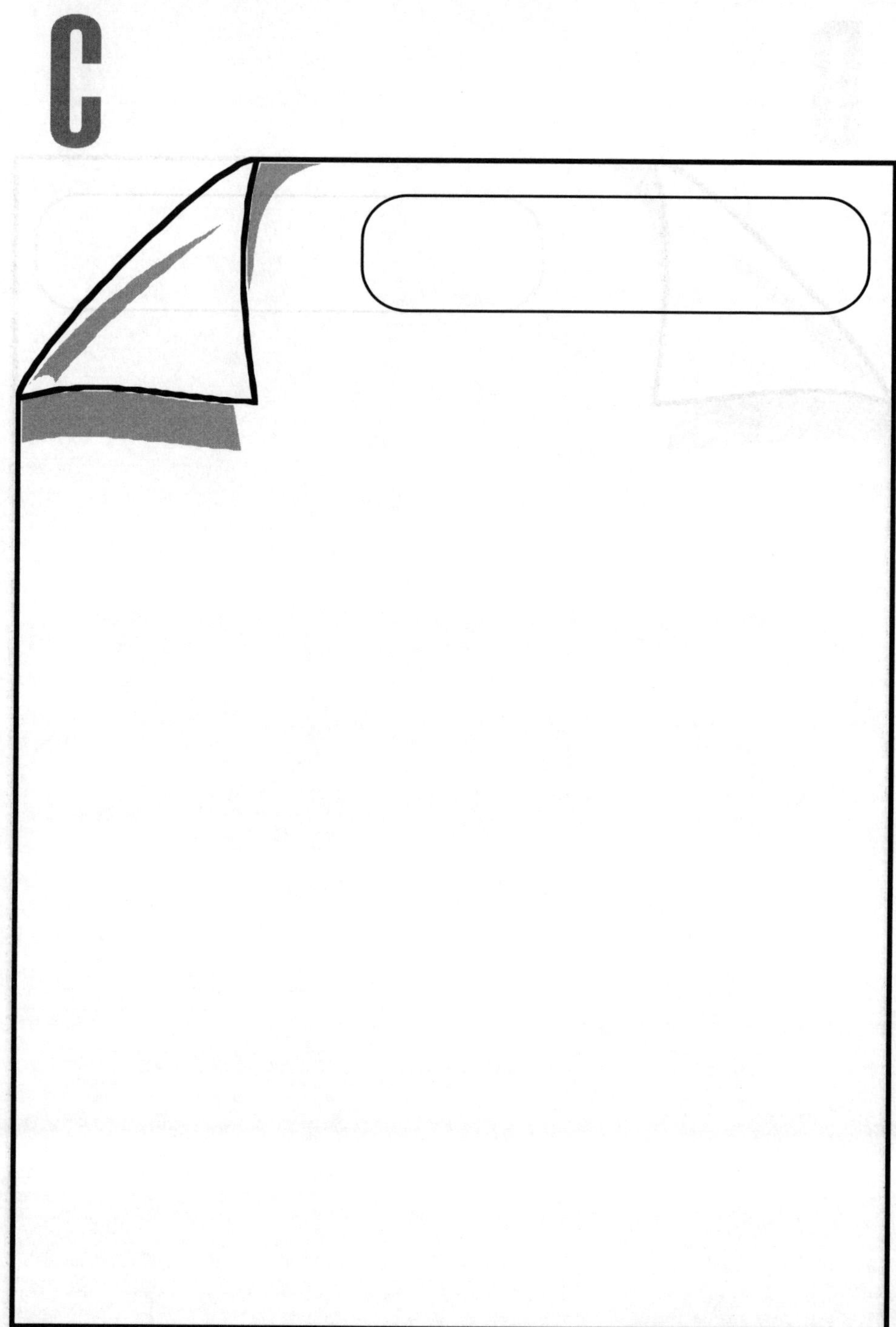

D

E

F

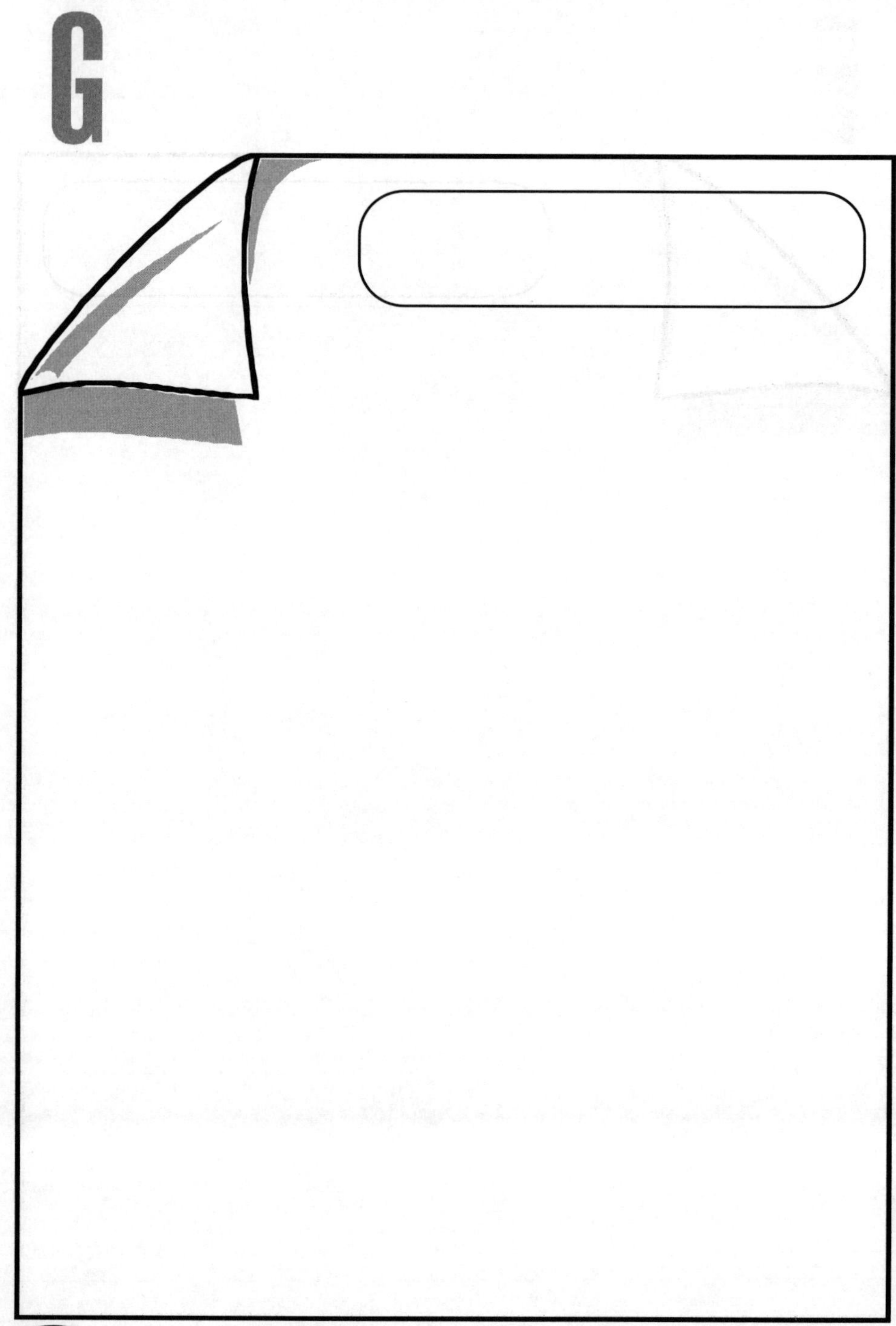
G

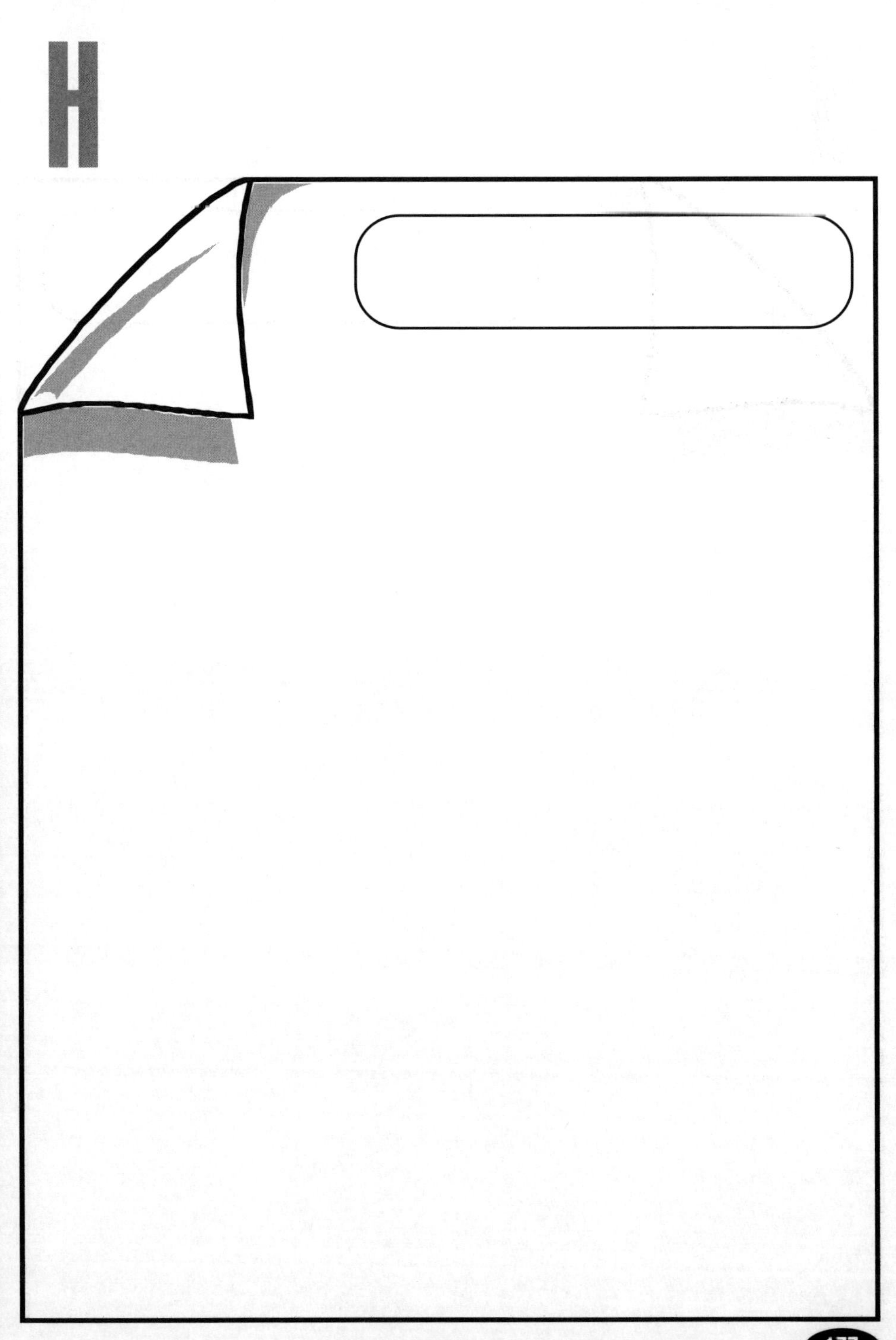

J

K

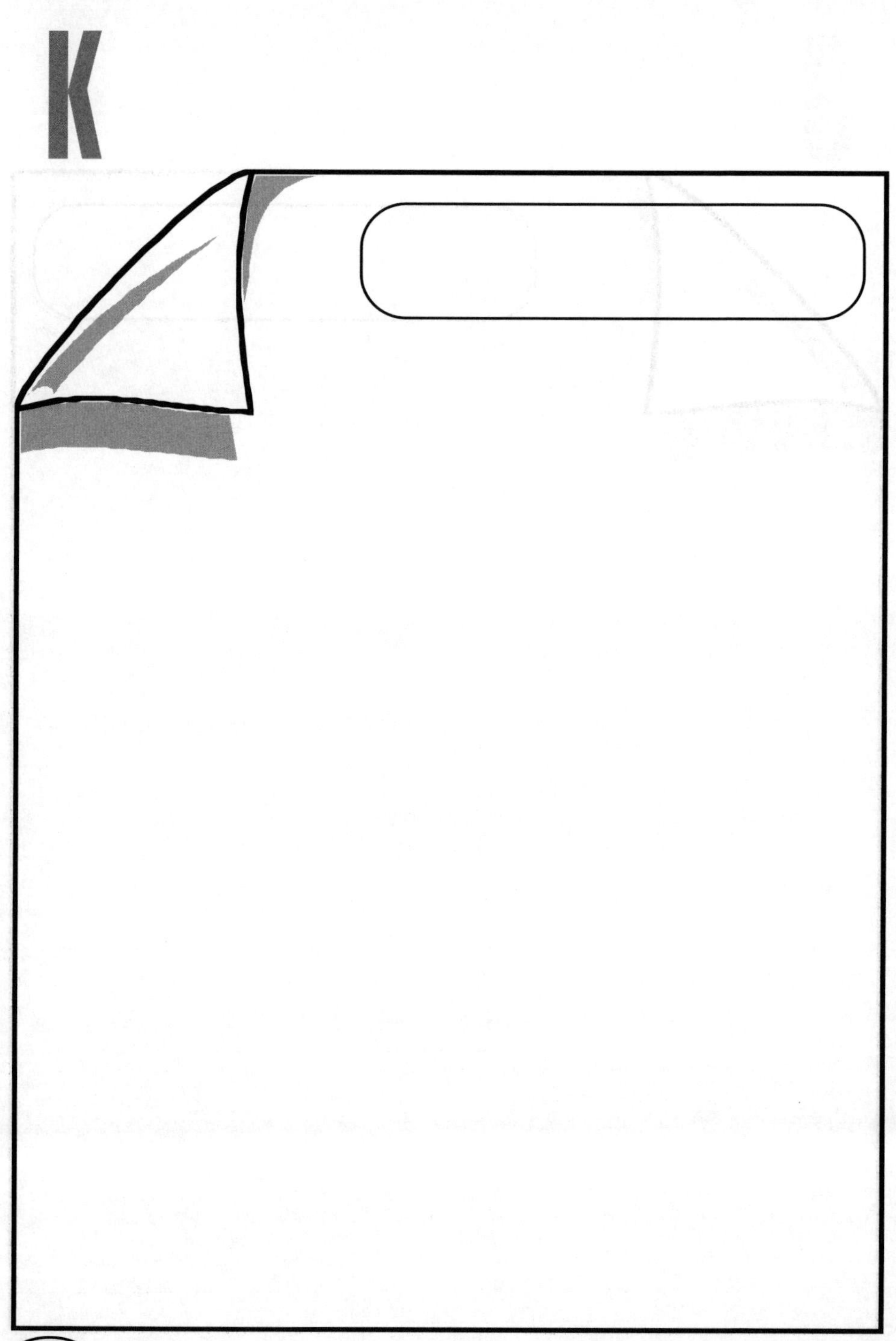

L

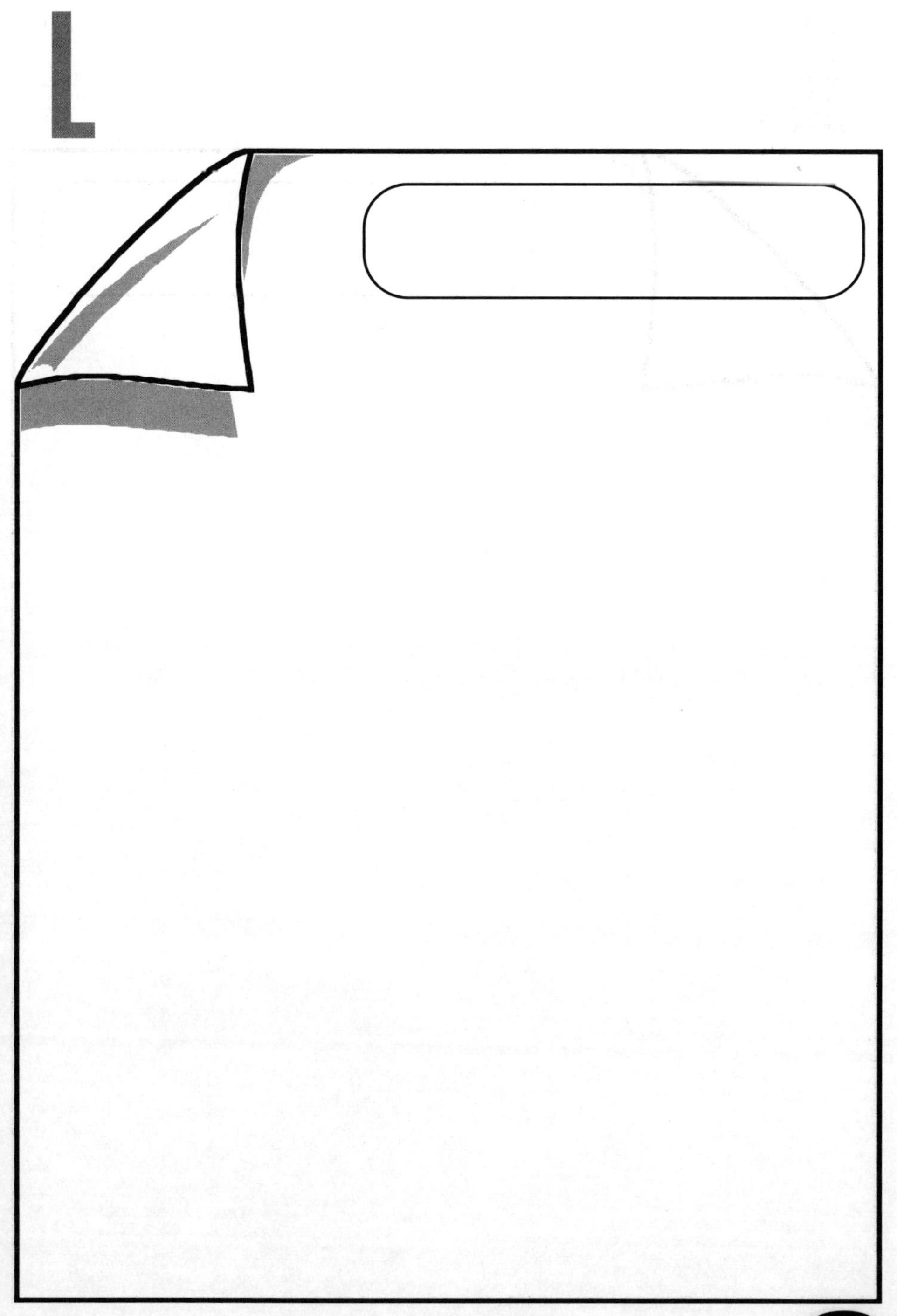

M

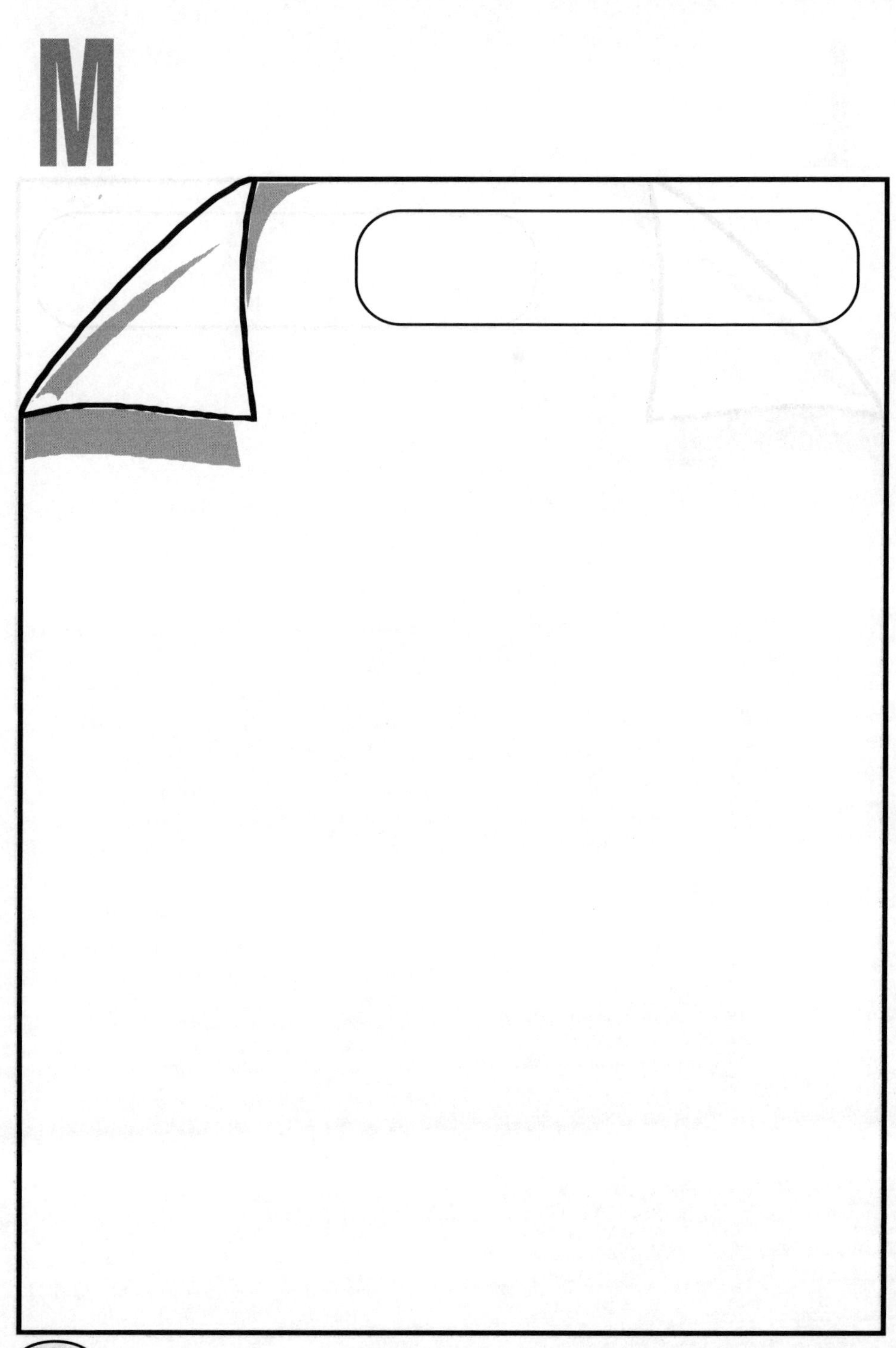

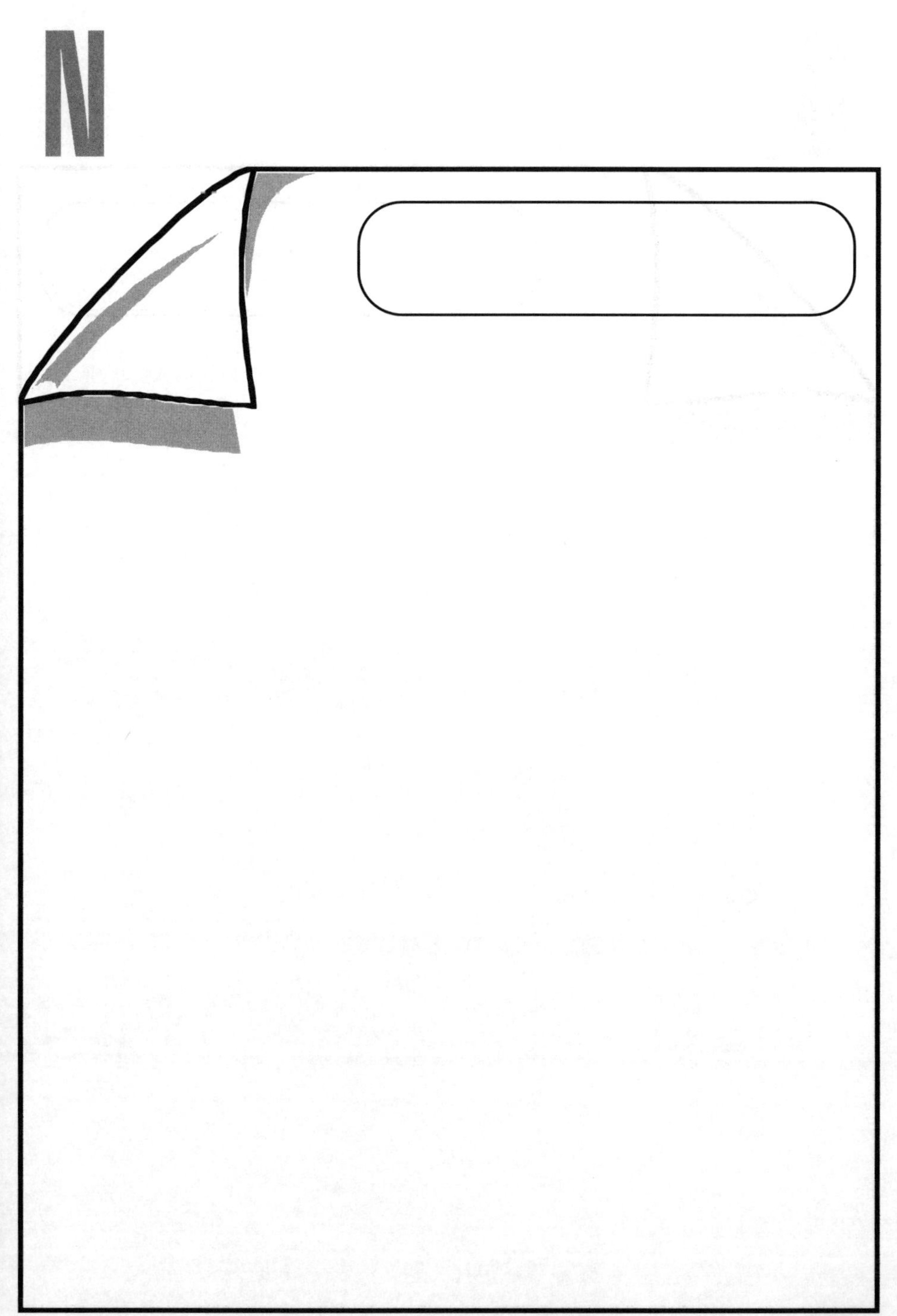
N

O

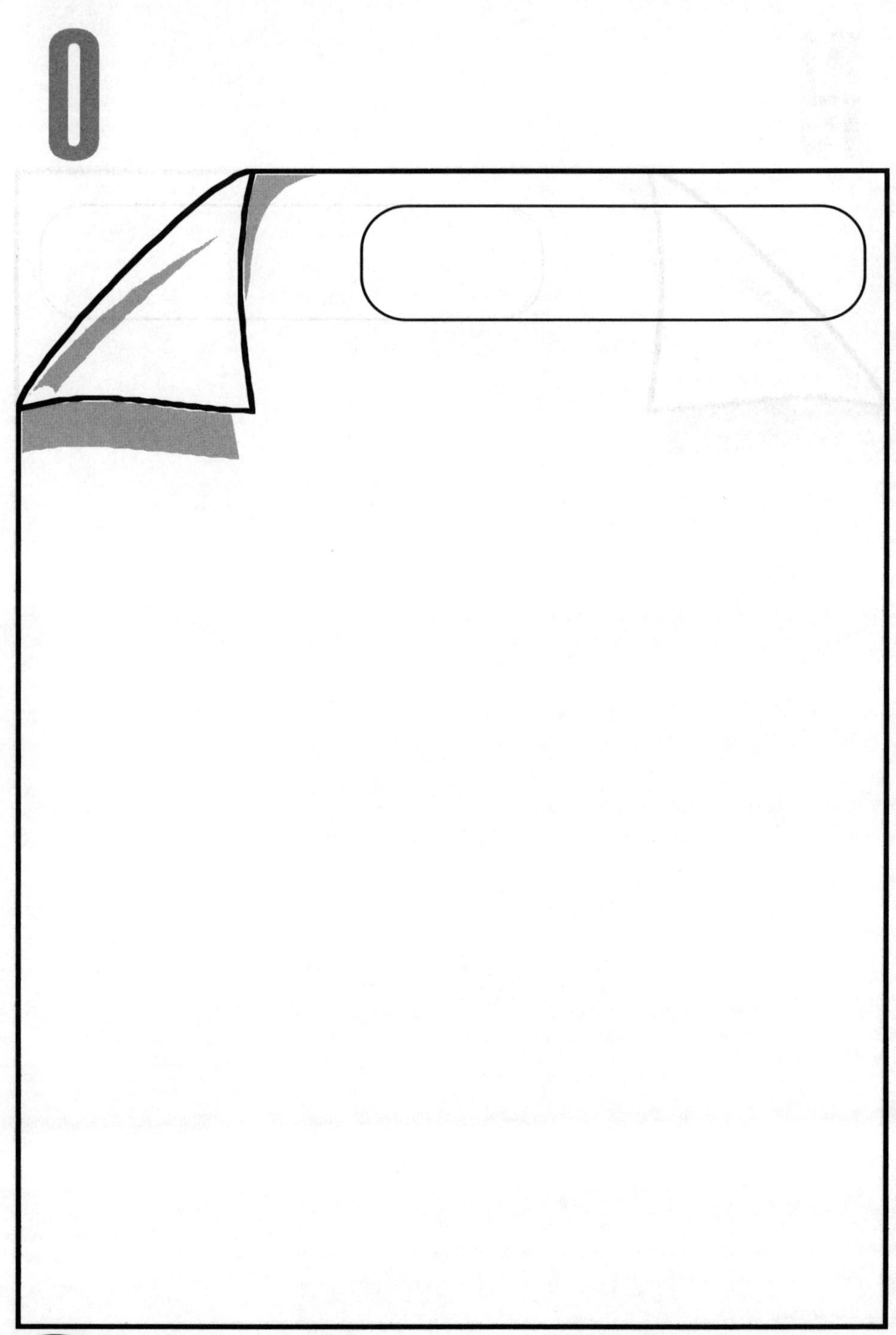

P

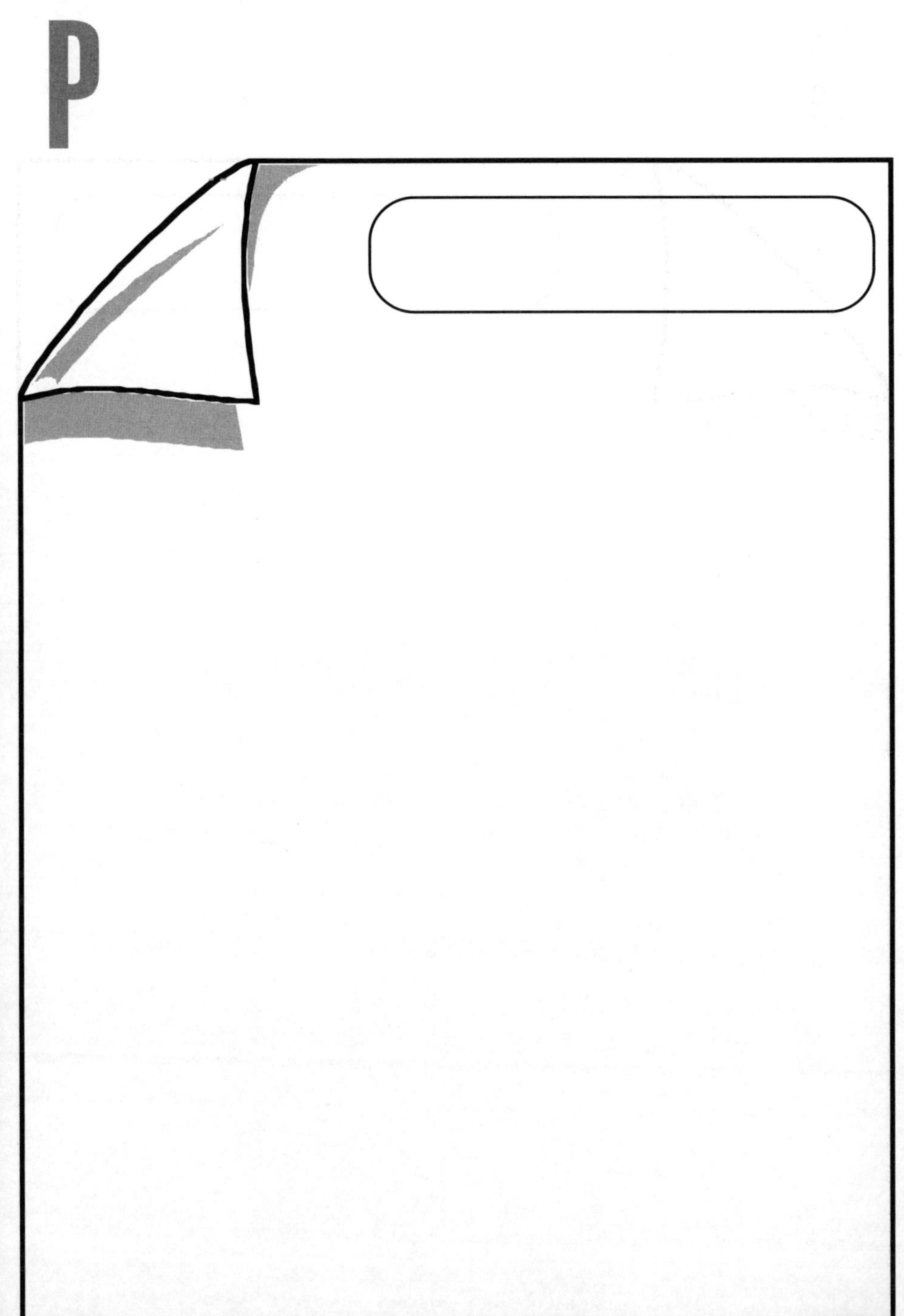

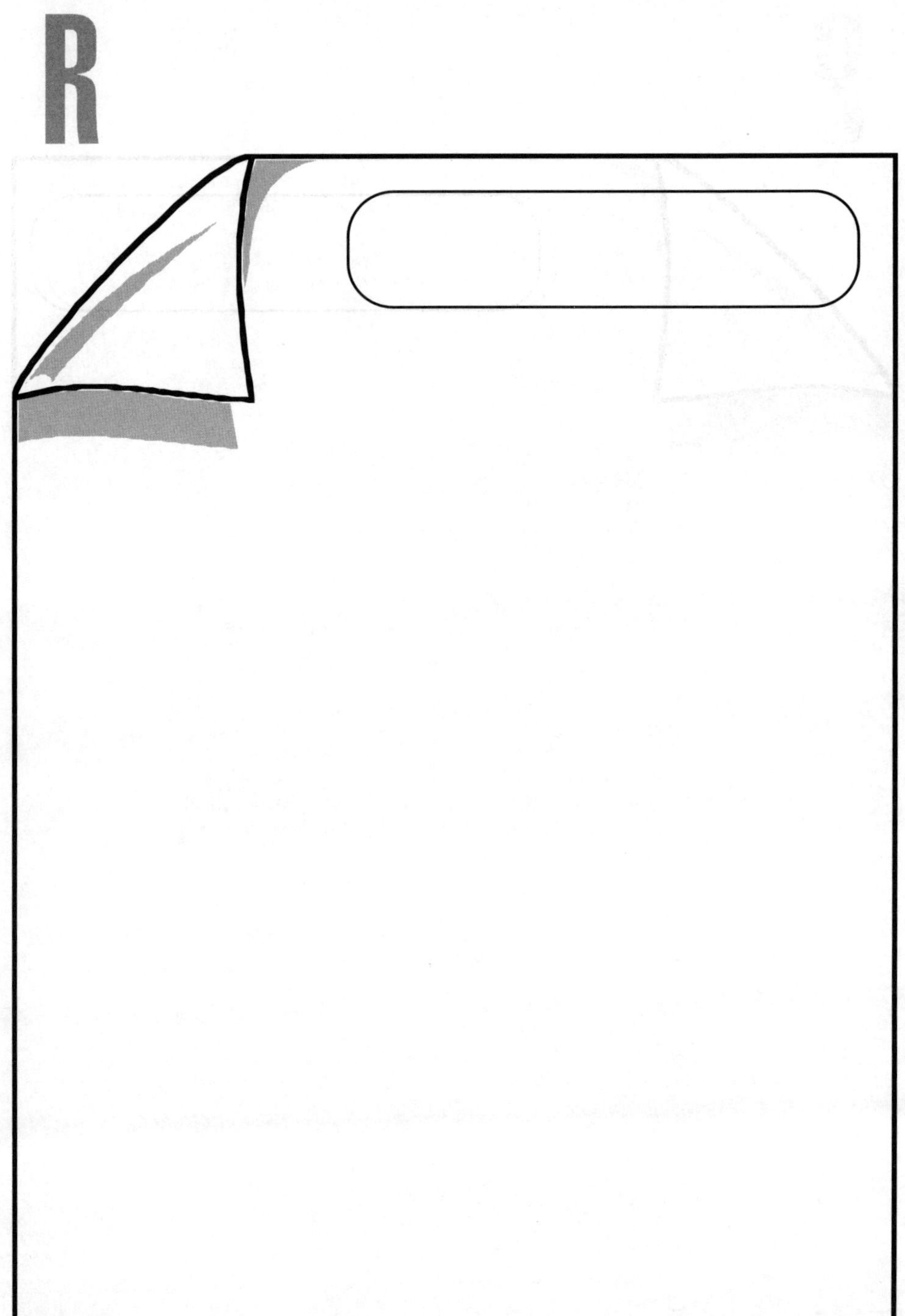
R

S

Shield

Who use's A Sheild

A Shield as you know is something which a Solder or someone in the army would have.

What's it for

A shield is used the protect you, for if someone threw or shot something at you, you would put your shield up and it would protect you.

people used shields in bible times to.

T

Treason

Where can I find it

In EXODUS 20 V4 you will see this word images. The above word treason as the same meaning as it does in the verse 4.

What does it mean

well verse 4 of EXODUS 20 is the secound commandment. It is telling us that we should only wharship god and god alone no images and that is what this word treason means.

How can I use it

we should remmber that we should never be treason towards god.

U

V

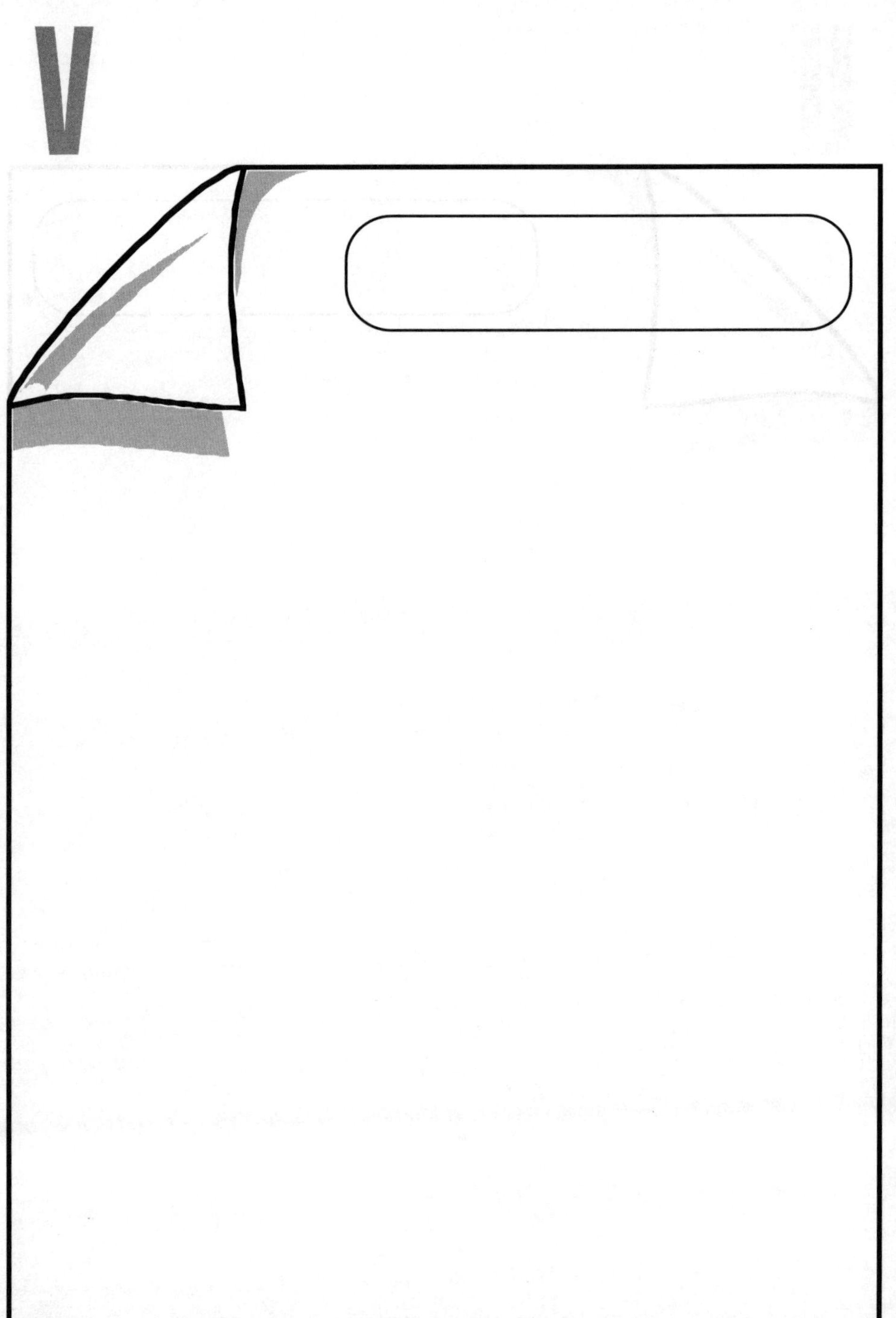

W

Y

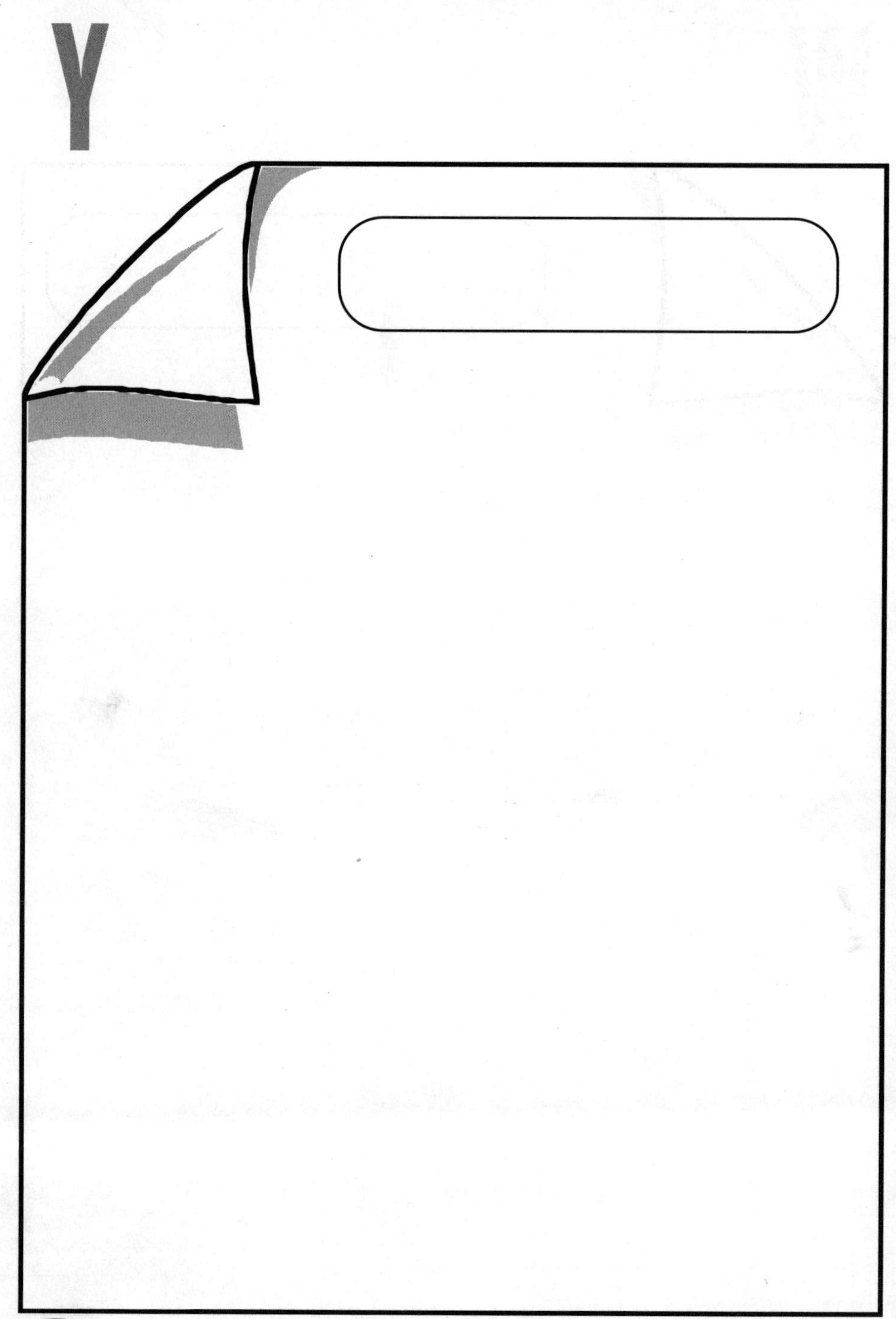